DRIED
FLOWER
GARDENING

DRIED FLOWER
GARDENING

Joanna Sheen
Caroline Alexander

WARD LOCK

To our children:
Pippa
Lorna, Thomas and Crispin

First published 1991 by Ward Lock
Villiers House, 41/47 Strand, London WC2N 5JE, England

A Cassell imprint

© Text and illustrations Ward Lock Limited 1991

Photography by Mike Evans
Illustrations by Tony Randell

Typeset in Goudy Old Style 11/12½ point
by Columns of Reading

Printed and bound in Spain by Graficromo

British Library Cataloguing in Publication Data
Sheen, Joanna
    Dried flower gardening.
    1. Gardens. Ornamental flowering plants. Cultivation
    I. Title   II. Alexander, Caroline
    635.9

ISBN 0–7063–6955–6

*Frontispiece: Air-drying can be a very
decorative method of preserving flowers.*

CONTENTS

INTRODUCTION 6

PLANNING YOUR CROP 8

HARVESTING AND DRYING 34

THE A–Z OF RECOMMENDED PLANTS 45

DRIED FLOWER ARRANGING 100

APPENDICES 120

INDEX 126

ACKNOWLEDGEMENTS 128

INTRODUCTION

Traditionally, dried flowers have been associated with autumnal and winter flower arrangements, to replace the fresh flowers of summer as they become less easily available. One often saw displays in muted shades of orange and brown, with some sun-bleached wheat or corn giving an overall effect of a faded, lifeless arrangement. Standards have changed dramatically in the last few years. Drying techniques have improved, the colours have become more vibrant and the choice much wider, and so the popularity of dried flowers has increased.

Commercially dried flowers are often dyed a range of bright and unnatural colours and are usually fairly expensive. The alternative, of growing and drying flowers at home, is far less intricate than one might have thought, and excellent results can be achieved by following the simple guidelines and harvesting information given in the following chapters. Many of the most expensive varieties in the shops are, in fact, the easiest to grow in your own garden, and very reliable to dry, so large savings can be made very quickly. What's more, a tremendous amount of satisfaction can be gained by growing the flowers from seed or a cutting, then harvesting and drying them for a finished arrangement in the home.

Many of the varieties mentioned in the A–Z section of this book may well be plants that are already established in your garden, or annuals that you have grown before, so you will quickly be able to start experimenting. Do take careful note of the instructions in the A–Z section, as there is a vast difference between a good specimen picked at the right time and dried in the correct manner, and a piece of plant material picked at random and abandoned to dry out! Once you have achieved the high standards that can be gained with a little care, your enthusiasm will soon increase. Then you will have to beware the 'drying bug' that can take over and make every available spot in the house overflow with plants and flowers of every description!

A bouquet of dried flowers, with such vibrant hues they could almost have been freshly picked from the garden.

Planning Your Crop

Many of the varieties that can be successfully dried are already popular garden choices, such as hydrangeas, eucalyptus, Chinese lanterns or peonies, and they may already be growing in your garden. There are several ways to tackle growing plants for drying purposes: you can harvest the plants you are already growing, plan a special area within the garden in which you will solely grow plants for drying, or combine the two by placing suitable plants throughout the garden, so the gaps created by the picked flowers are less obvious.

By taking note of when a plant is to be harvested, you can plan the more visible areas of your garden to house such plants as poppies, love-in-a-mist and honesty, all of which are picked at the seed pod stage and therefore give maximum enjoyment before they are removed from the garden and dried. Many species, such as *Achillea ptarmica*, can be harvested in small amounts as they flower, thereby leaving other flowers to develop on the plant. There are others that would be suitable for fairly prominent positions, such as hydrangeas and *A. filipendulina*, that are harvested late in flowering and so give a good show before they are removed! Obviously any plants that need cutting very early in the flowering stage, such as *Helichrysum* and golden rod, *Solidago*, should be sited in an inconspicuous spot as they will never look their best.

Apart from planning the visual aspects of the garden, you also need to choose which flowers you wish to grow and which ones may be better left off your list, and instead bought either ready dried or in fresh bunches from a florist so you can dry them yourself. Although old-fashioned roses dry beautifully and are an important asset to any arranger's collection, if you want to use a reasonably large amount of roses it is far better to buy bunches of fresh roses when they are at their cheapest and dry them for use later. Commercially grown roses usually have small heads but far longer stems, and so are useful in large arrangements.

Dried roses are a marvellous asset, when you are arranging your collection of dried flowers and foliages. Really generous amounts of roses used in an arrangement look very effective, and have good strong colour and shape.

Growing background material

Where possible you should try to grow plant material of as many shapes and sizes as possible. Background material, such as foliage for glycerining, grasses or less spectacular items, which provide blocks of colour, are just as important as prize specimens for the centre of the arrangement! As seasoned dried flower arrangers will appreciate, it takes quite a large quantity of material to fill an arrangement, and so stocks of good-quality background material or fillers, such as sea lavender, *Alchemilla*, *Achillea* 'Cerise Queen' or hydrangea heads, are a tremendous help when you come to making up your arrangements. Remember, too, the scale of plant material you are preserving: if the vast majority is ideal for miniature flower arrangements, apart from one or two hydrangea heads and a giant *Allium* head, then it is unlikely that you will use the larger material, such as *Allium* heads and *Moluccella*, at all. So balance the size of material you grow and aim towards a good spread of flowers and leaves, so you will have plenty of flexibility and scope when you come to arrange your harvest.

Other background items that are particularly helpful for filling out arrangements include lavender (the larger headed varieties and darker colourings are preferable), Carthamus, a strong thistle shape which has a soft green colouring when picked in bud, and *Achillea ptarmica* (The Pearl), which usually keeps its good clear white and is very useful for lightening dark or drab arrangements.

Growing requirements

Soil types must also come into your calculations. If a particular plant needs soil that differs from that in your garden it is unlikely to prosper, so concentrate on growing more tolerant plants or those that are ideally suited to the soil conditions that you have. Generally speaking, your soil type does not need to be good as many varieties flower happily on poorer or slightly impoverished soils, but rainfall or irrigation is essential for many varieties to achieve good stem length and, of course, the acidity of the soil is critical for some species and also influences the colour of hydrangea heads. (Alkaline soils produce pink flower heads and acid soils produce blue ones.) These guidelines also apply to problems with varieties that are sensitive to climatic conditions and have special drying requirements: it is far better to ignore these varieties unless you have the correct conditions to produce quality specimens. Consider carefully where you are going to display your dried flowers and avoid damp atmospheres or bright sunlight. *Helichrysum bracteatum* and *Limonium sinuatum* hold their colour better than most varieties in direct light. Some varieties mentioned in the A–Z section, particularly *Helichrysum*, are more likely to re-absorb moisture than others and will have to be wired to ensure they don't droop once in an arrangement, so if you prefer not to fiddle with wires you should not grow such plants.

ANNUALS

Annuals can be a very satisfying group of plants to grow in the garden, as they are relatively easy to raise and success is probably assured. They are ready to harvest within the same season and so help overcome one's impatience to see instant results. There are many sources for seeds, both by mail order and from shops and garden centres, and a large and useful crop can be raised from a reasonably small outlay on seeds.

Annuals can be sown to infill spaces within a flowerbed or can be given their own area. In a few months you can have a riot of colour, which can all be directed towards drying and preserving, or some plants can be grown for colour and some for cutting. Wonderful colour schemes can be created with annuals so rapidly, you can have broad strokes of warm reds with deep greens or lime greens. The pinks always blend beautifully with the silvers and greys but try adding dark blue and purple for a stunning effect.

As you can see from the collection shown here, there is a multitude of colours and shapes and sizes available, so the only constraint is time and space for drying.

A brilliantly-coloured array of annual plants that dry well and can be grown quickly.

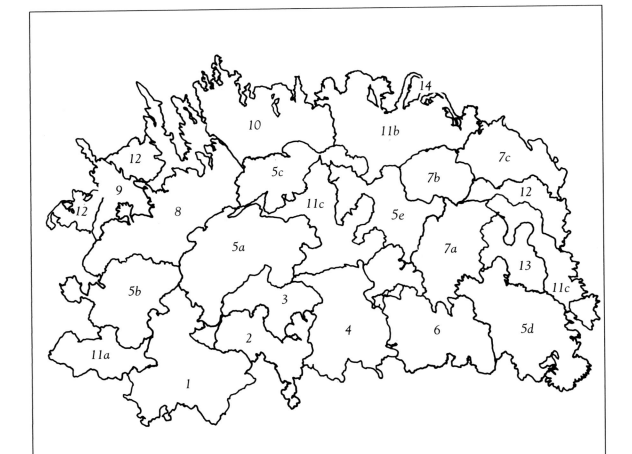

Annuals

1 *Origanum dictamnus*

2 *Ammobium alatum*

3 *Tagetes erecta*

4 *Limonium suworowii*

5a *Helichrysum bracteatum monstrosum* (salmon)

5b *Helichrysum* (lemon yellow)

5c *Helichrysum* (silver rose)

5d *Helichrysum* (cream)

5e *Helichrysum* (purple)

6 *Lonas inodora*

7a *Limonium sinuatum* (pink)

7b *Limonium sinuatum* (apricot)

7c *Limonium sinuatum* (mixed)

8 *Xeranthemum annuum*

9 *Amaranthus paniculatus* (red)

10 *Delphinium elatum*

11a *Carthamus tinctorius* (closed bud stage)

11b *Carthamus tinctorius* (orange)

11c *Carthamus tinctorius* (cream)

12 *Acroclinium roseum*

13 *Aster sp.*

14 *Ambrosinia mexicana*

Colour schemes

Colour should be another consideration when choosing plants: if you know you will want a particular colour bias then you should incorporate it into your planting scheme. Later in this chapter you will find several planting schemes that are planned around various colours, and they may form a useful basis for your own decisions. Once your enthusiasm has grown then you may wish to grow everything you can, but if space or time is limited it seems logical to concentrate on particular flowers or colours that will be of most use. Contrasts are just as important as co-ordinating colours. For example, even if your interior colours have a very strong pink, cream or peach colour theme, do allocate some space to plants with stronger, deeper colours, such as *Amaranthus*, as the strong dark red shows off the paler colours very effectively and you will have a far more stunning arrangement if you can include some darker colours as well. Clashing colours can also give a vibrant effect – for instance, red roses against a pink background – and remember that using bright greens in arrangements always helps them to look fresh.

GROWING ANNUALS

Annuals are a useful choice for drying as they are fast-growing and, if you are impatient as most of us are, then you will be pleased at the quick results that can be harvested and used within a single season. Do remember, however, that many annuals have a fairly critical picking time, so you must be prepared to watch them closely to ensure best results. Another problem can be rain that falls just when a crop is ready to pick, and this can often seriously damage its quality. One way round this problem is to stagger the sowing of annuals so that, with luck, some will escape any weather problems. When choosing varieties to sow, pick types with the maximum amount of flowers on a spike or flower head. The plants with closely spaced or double flowers are more suitable than sparser varieties. Depth or strength of colour is also important as many colours will intensify with drying but do eventually fade.

Many varieties can be sown direct into the garden, but some, such as *Craspedia* and *Gomphrena* need to be raised in trays and planted out. This system can also be useful for establishing popular plants, such as *Helichrysum* as early as possible so as to achieve an extended harvesting period later in the year.

Should your enthusiasm grow to the point where you want larger quantities of your particular favourite, then a separate area could be laid out much like a vegetable garden. This is also a help where plants may need staking or support, such as cornflower or Bells of Ireland. In such plots, facilities for watering during establishment will probably be necessary and weed control will be a continual problem. The only viable solution is to sow the seeds into as clean a seed-bed as possible and to keep the area hand-weeded or hoed at regular intervals throughout the growing season.

Helichrysum and Statice

The ever-popular *Helichrysum* and Statice (*Limonium sinuatum*) are both fast-growing annuals. They have traditionally formed the basis for many arrangements and can be grown in a wide range of long-lasting colours. Both bloom successfully over a long period, but whereas *Helichrysum* is picked at an early stage and is probably best suited to an inconspicuous plot of its own, Statice is not harvested until it has reached full flower and so can make a valuable contribution to the flower border. The deep purple *Helichrysum* shown in the photograph on page 10 is a wonderful foil to the apricot and pink Statice, especially when arranged in small bunches rather than single stems.

Larkspur

Whatever your particular choice of colour, *Delphinium consolida*, or larkspur, is a must. Larkspur looks attractive growing as a traditional cottage garden plant and dries beautifully. You can grow plants in several shades of pink running into mauves and lilacs, pale blues, striking deep blues and white. It is easy to grow and even after the main stems have been harvested, the side shoots will provide a supply of shorter flower heads ideal for smaller arrangements.

Herbs

It is worth experimenting with all sorts of aromatic plants but, of the annual herbs, *Origanum dictamnus* and dill are among the most useful for arrangements. Oregano is a useful filler, being a soft sage-green colour, and dill has a delicate flower head.

Nigella

Of the various annuals grown for their seed heads, *Nigella* or Love-in-a-mist is one of the most popular. With its delicate form and interesting green and dark red markings, it blends with most colour schemes and is very versatile in its use. Both the flowers and the seed pods are equally attractive in the garden and then it self-seeds readily for the following year!

GROWING PERENNIALS

Perennials are a worthwhile investment in any garden, though the initial outlay may be higher on purchasing plants, rather than seeds. Patience is needed as it may take several years for plants to flower in harvestable quantities.

Sea Lavender

Two types of sea lavender are shown in the photograph on pages 16–17 — *Limonium tartaricum dumosa*, familiar to all flower arrangers as an excellent filler, and the finer *Limonium latifolium*. The quality of sea lavender can easily be marred by crushing when packed; the home-grown bunches can be allowed to retain their natural spreading form and thus will be very attractive to use.

The *Achillea* Family

The *Achillea* family provides several useful flower types. The yellow *A. filipendulina* is easy to grow, long-lasting in flower and sturdy to use. *A. millefolium* 'Cerise Queen' and the more recently introduced 'Summer Pastels' are excellent plants to off-set stronger or brighter colours, and *A. ptarmica*, 'The Pearl', is worth growing for its masses of creamy-white flowers on tall strong stems.

Peonies, Globe thistles and Delphiniums

Peonies are a wonderful asset in the garden because the flowers are expensive to buy and not readily available. They can give a glorious touch of distinction as focal points in dried arrangements. Globe thistles, *Echinops*, are also worthy of cultivation but need gentle handling. They are a wonderful steely blue and have a distinctive textural feel. Dried delphiniums are rarely available commercially; the sparkling dark blue spikes and even the paler blues dry well and are very useful in large arrangements.

Lavender and Herbs

Lavender is a plant that no dried flower enthusiast should be without as there are so many uses for it, whether in pot pourri, scented sachets or as bunches in displays. Other scented plants, particularly herbs, are increasing in popularity and many can be glycerined as well as air-dried. Perennial marjoram has a marvellous pink or dark purple colour, thymes and mints have a pleasant fragrance, bay leaves are useful in small wreaths or table centre decorations and the delicate spires of *Ambrosinia* have a lemony scent that can pervade a whole

(continued on p. 18)

15

PERENNIALS

The perennials illustrated are a colourful array, ranging from humble chives to sophisticated peonies and from tiny *Gypsophila* flowers to large hydrangea heads.

Many perennial plants are magnificent centrepieces for your arrangements as well as useful padding, which may not be such a starring role but is of equal importance. Structural and textural material is essential as components in a dried flower basket.

All varieties of *Achillea* are useful, mainly as fillers or background material. The *filipendulina* form is a strong yellow that makes a good contrast to royal purples and mauves, heather for example. The dark pink 'Cerise Queen' is excellent with all the pinks, and blues. The green *Agastache* has insignificant white flowers which shrivel to leave a soft mid-green that mixes with the majority of colour themes. *Agastache* also smells deliciously minty.

Hydrangeas and peonies whether they are fresh or dried look magnificent and cannot be too highly recommended. The pink variety of peonies in the photograph is 'Sarah Bernhardt', which holds its colour very well. Hydrangeas are relatively easy to grow and the colour can be manipulated, if necessary.

Wonderful colours and shapes are available in this selection of perennial plants.

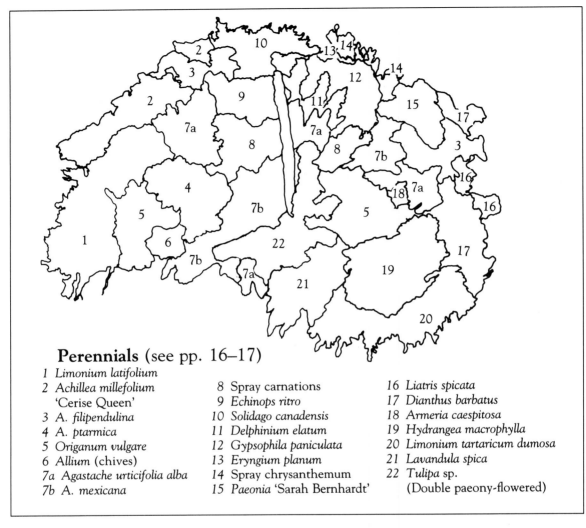

Perennials (see pp. 16–17)

1 *Limonium latifolium*
2 *Achillea millefolium*
  'Cerise Queen'
3 *A. filipendulina*
4 *A. ptarmica*
5 *Origanum vulgare*
6 *Allium* (chives)
7a *Agastache urticifolia alba*
7b *A. mexicana*

8 Spray carnations
9 *Echinops ritro*
10 *Solidago canadensis*
11 *Delphinium elatum*
12 *Gypsophila paniculata*
13 *Eryngium planum*
14 Spray chrysanthemum
15 *Paeonia* 'Sarah Bernhardt'

16 *Liatris spicata*
17 *Dianthus barbatus*
18 *Armeria caespitosa*
19 *Hydrangea macrophylla*
20 *Limonium tartaricum dumosa*
21 *Lavandula spica*
22 *Tulipa* sp.
  (Double paeony-flowered)

room when touched. Two more unusual plants to be recommended are *Agastache mexicana* with its blue-flowered spike and *A. urticifolia alba* which has a white flower, but dries to give a pale green spike. Both are aromatic and the subtle colourings extremely useful. The leaves can be used in pot pourri (see the recipes at the end of the book). *Helichrysum italicum* or *H. angustifolium*, otherwise known as the curry plant (for obvious reasons if one smells the foliage) is a particular favourite as the silver foliage gives a visual lift to an arrangement and is so dainty. The flowers are also useful and the shrub is evergreen so adds colour to the garden when it needs it most.

Sage, fennel, dill, rosemary and many others all have their contribution to make, and it is worth remembering that if a plant has a lovely scent, it does not matter if its appearance is somewhat dull. It can be tucked into the back or sides of a container, out of sight, but still appreciated!

GARDEN FLOWERS

This display of garden flowers includes a range of annuals, perennials and herbs, all of which can be grown and dried at home, but many of which are not readily available to purchase commercially. Textures range from the delicate green Alchemilla and white Matricaria through to the strong, dramatic forms of the yellow Craspedia (drumsticks) and Centaurea (Knapweed) and the red Celosia (Cockscomb) and peonies. Hops and Euphorbia provide a useful source of green, instead of grasses, and the leaves of peonies and roses should always be kept as background filler material. The grey leaves of Senecio are attractive, even though they tend to curl up when dried, and the small white and yellow flowers of Anaphalis are delightfully soft and delicate to use. Unusual pastel shades can be provided by stocks and asters, which can add colour to arrangements.

SEED HEADS

Some of the most beautiful plant forms to dry are the various seed heads and similar items that fall into this category. This is an obvious bonus in the garden as you can enjoy the plants for longer before they have to be harvested, but also the seed heads give texture and interest to arrangements. There are many sizes and types from which to choose and as you can see from the photograph opposite, the strength and variety of colour is amazing.

Poppy heads are very attractive and also useful as their colour ranges from slate blue to grey, green and beige. Another really dramatic head to use is the globe artichoke, *Cynara scolymus*, particularly when it is fully open, as seen in the central example in the picture. It gives a strong focal point to any design. Chinese lanterns, *Physalis franchettii*, are another very popular choice. Their orange colouring is very vivid and gives a warm glow to arrangements.

All the seed heads, such as linseed and, in particular, *Allium christophii*, look wonderful sprayed with metallic paints for festive arrangements at Christmas. Whatever shade you use, the effect is very beautiful and so simply achieved. Obviously within this group one can also include all the cones, which can be wired to use in arrangements or displayed decoratively in bowls, perhaps with pot pourri (see pp. 114–17).

Seed Heads

1 *Typha latifolia*
2 *Allium sp.* (Leek flower heads)
3 *Cynara scolymus*
4 *Cynara cardunculus*
5 *Acanthus mollis*
6 *Physalis franchettii*
7 *Papaver somniferum*
8 *Allium christophii*
9 *Linum usitatissium*
10 *Nigella damascena*
11 *Eucalyptus gunnii*
12 *Centaurea macrocephala*
13 *Phlomis* 'Edward Bowles'
14 *Aquilegia hybrida*
15 *Sedum spectabile*
16 *Alnus glutinosa*
17 *Papaver sp.*
18 *Lunaria biennis*
19 *Iris foetidissima*
20 *Dipsacus fullonum*
21 *Fagus sylvatica*
22 *Lepidium ruderale*
23 *Anethum graveolens*

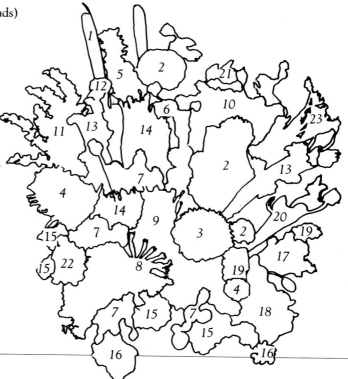

Seed heads can range from small and nondescript to the more exotic artichokes and Allium heads.

ROSES AND PEONIES

Although many forms of rose dry well, there are several varieties that lose their colour quite quickly, such as the pale yellow and pale pink forms. Reds darken dramatically during drying but then hold their colour well. You will need to experiment with your garden varieties to see which work best for you. The photograph opposite includes the commercial rose varieties 'Gerdo', 'Bridal Pink' and 'Porcelina', as well as the garden favourites 'Schoolgirl', 'Blue Moon', 'Iceberg' and many other garden varieties. In order to get the stem length for larger arrangements, give garden varieties false wire stems covered with green florist's tape.

Also shown in the photograph opposite are red, cream and pink peonies. Peonies are among the most attractive flowers to dry, and although the drying process makes them shrink, they can still have fabulous large heads and make any arrangement very special. Do take careful note of the details in the A–Z section regarding combating insect damage as it can be extremely disappointing to lose your best specimens in this way after they have dried out. If you have trouble mastering the technique of drying peonies, any fallen petals that result can easily be used in pot pourri or wedding confetti (see pp. 116–17 and p. 118).

Roses are fairly easy to dry and garden varieties can give excellent results.

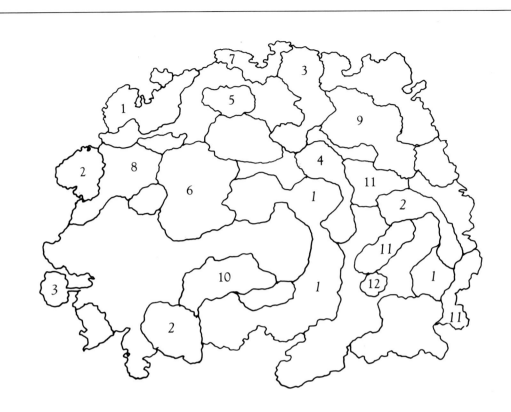

Roses and Peonies

1 *Paeonia* 'Sarah Bernhardt'
2 *Paeonia officinalis*
3 *Paeonia* 'Duchesse de Nemours'
4 *Rosa* 'Porcelina'
5 *Rosa* 'Golden Thyme'
6 *Rosa* 'Tamara'
7 *Rosa* 'Mercedes'
8 *Rosa* 'Jaguar'
9 *Rosa* 'Bridal Pink'
10 *Rosa* 'Minuet'
11 *Rosa* 'Gerdo'
12 *Rosa* 'Blue Moon'
plus a selection of garden roses

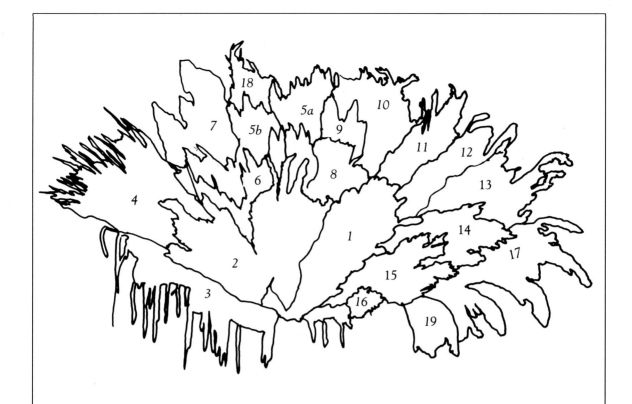

Grasses

1 *Lagurus ovatus*
2 *Zea mays*
3 *Carex pendula*
4 *Triticale*
5a *Triticum* (early harvest)
5b *Triticum* (late harvest)
6 *Phleum pratense*
7 *Cortaderia selloana*
8 *Festuca ovina*
9 *Hordeum*
10 *Avena sativa*
11 *Setaria italica*
12 *Phalaris canariensis*

13 *Cynosurus cristata*
14 *Bromus macrostachys*
15 *Poa annua*
16 *Briza maxima*
17 *Panicum miliaceum*
18 *Dactylis glomerata*
19 *Bromus sterilis*

GRASSES

Grasses are among the easiest plants to obtain for drying, although some of the showier specimens will need special cultivation. There are a great many varieties to choose from. Cereal crops such as wheat and oats have distinctive heads and can add impact to an arrangement, particularly if used in large clumps rather than inserted stem by stem. Fescue or quaking grass give a much daintier effect.

Millet has a variety of shapes, sizes and colours, some upright and some in a pendulous form, and a range of colours from gold through to green. Pampas grass has also always been a favourite but it can be very overwhelming unless used subtly in large arrangements.

Grasses are not expensive to buy ready-dried but are, surprisingly, one of the most difficult items to dry successfully at home since their all-important greenness is only retained by fast drying. Only a minimum amount of space should be allocated to growing the common varieties in the garden. On the other hand, certain ornamental varieties make interesting contrasts as clumps in the herbaceous border. Rather than just sowing one or two types of grass, mixed packets of flower arrangers' grasses are available, which give a better breadth of choice.

There are enormous numbers of grasses, both wild and cultivated, which add a feathery touch to any arrangement.

IDEAS FOR PLANTING SCHEMES

Having decided to incorporate flowers and plants for drying in your garden plan, there are several ways in which this can be done. One of the most interesting is to plant in colour themes, which provides a good colour co-ordinated selection of dried flowers to work with as well as giving pleasure while the plants are growing. There are several ideas in the following pages which can either be followed exactly or taken as a base for using some of the plants you may have already and adding some new ideas.

A theme which would be fun to work on would be a wild garden. It should not be so wild that the plants within it are allowed to take over, but rather is an apparently unstructured garden.

Plants chosen for a wild or woodland garden need to be those that flourish well with little or no interference. Avoid any that need staking or tying up. There should be a minimum of annual replanting so as to disturb the soil as little as possible.

Plants can happily be grown in tubs and containers as well as in beds. The following list does not place emphasis on any particular colour, but all the plants are very useful for drying, as well as being attractive in their own right. The list includes scented and evergreen plants and herbs (also grown for their culinary use), as well as plants that are harvested late in the flowering season or at seed-head stage and which can therefore be enjoyed to the full in the garden.

Suitable plants for patios and smaller gardens

Acroclinium roseum (Sunray)
Alchemilla mollis (Lady's mantle)
Aquilegia hybrida
Calendula officinalis (Pot marigold)
Centaurea cyanus (Cornflower)
Clematis tangutica
Dahlia sp.
Helichrysum angustifolium (Curry plant)
Hydrangea sp.
Lavandula spica (Lavender)

Limonium sinuatum (Statice)
Limonium tartaricum dumosa
Nigella damascena
Origanum vulgare (Pot marjoram)
Thymus (Thyme)
Xeranthemum annuum

Pink, Green and White

Here the many varied tones of pink are complemented by the mauves and blues of *Liatris*, cornflower and larkspur. The clumps of grasses provide a different texture and the white *Achillea* and sea lavender give useful highlights. The overall effect can be a beautiful swathe of subtle shades which would look restful as well as being a lovely garden feature.

PERENNIAL

1 *Achillea ptarmica*
2 *Achillea millefolium*
3 *Aster novae-belgii* (purple)
4 *Liatris spicata*
5 *Dianthus barbatus*
6 *Dianthus x. allwoodii*
7 *Gypsophila paniculata*
8 *Limonium tartaricum dumosa*
9 *Alchemilla molis*
10 *Paeonia lactiflora* 'Sarah Bernhardt'
11 *P. officinalis* (cerise)
12 *Limonium sinuatum* (pink, white, blue)
13 *Rosa* sp. (shrub, double pink)
14 *Sedum spectabile*

ANNUAL

15 *Acroclinium roseum* (white/pink)
16 *Amaranthus*
17 *Aster* (mixed pink/cerise)
18 *Centaurea cyanus* — mixed (pink, purple, blue)
19 *Delphinium consolida* (pink and blue)
20 *Gomphrena globosa* (purple)
21 *Helichrysum bracteatum monstrosum* (pink, purple and light pink)
22 *Limonium suworowii*
23 *Nigella damascena*
24 *Salvia horminum*
25 *Xeranthemum annuum* (white and purple)

GRASSES

26 *Phalaris canariensis*
27 *Miscanthus sinensis*

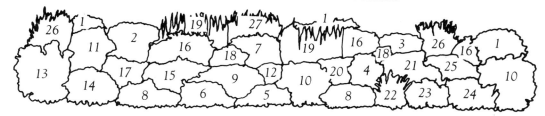

Red, Green, White

Several of the plants recommended in this scheme could be used in locations with light shade — in particular the *Euphorbia*, hellebores, hydrangeas and *Astrantia*. The bright reds are best contrasted with light greens and the scheme needs the highlights of *Achillea ptarmica*, clematis and chrysanthemum to provide interest.

PERENNIAL

1 *Acanthus mollis* or *A. spinosus*
2 *Achillea ptarmica*
3 *Alchemilla mollis*
4 *Aquilegia hybrida*
5 *Astilbe arendsii*
6 *Astrantia major*
7 *Hydrangea* sp.
*8 *Chrysanthemum* sp. (orange/yellow)
*9 *Clematis tangutica* or *C. orientalis*
10 *Corylus avellana contorta*
11 *Cotinus coggygria*
12 *Dianthus barbatus*

13 *Eucalyptus gunnii*
14 *Euphorbia polychroma*
15 *Helleborus corsicus*
16 *Hydrangea macrophylla*
17 *Hydrangea paniculatum* 'Grandiflora'
18 *Iris foetidissima*
19 *Lunaria biennis*
20 *Paeonia officinalis*
21 *Physalis franchettii*
22 *Rosa* sp. ('Variegati di Bologna')
23 *Rosa* sp. (double red rambler type)

* For contrast

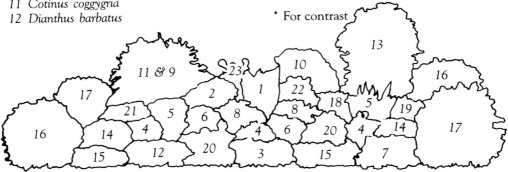

Orange, Yellow, White and Green

Strong oranges and yellows always look particularly good with deep reds and dark foliage. Here the rosemary, *Moluccella* and hellebores, plus the *Cotinus* and *Amaranthus* all work as background or contrast colours to what could be a dramatic scheme. The bright, warm colours could give life to an otherwise dull part of the garden.

PERENNIAL

1 *Alchemilla mollis*
2 *Achillea filipendulina*
3 *Centaurea macrocephala*
4 *Hydrangea paniculata* 'Grandiflora'
5 *Matricaria eximia*
6 *Phlomis* 'Edward Bowles'
7 *Physalis franchettii*
8 *Rosa* sp. (rambler, cream, double-flowered)
9 *Clematis tangutica* or *Clematis orientalis*
10 *Helleborus corsicus*
11 *Solidago canadensis*
12 *Kerria japonica*
13 *Agastache urticifolia alba*
14 *Cotinus coggygria* 'Foliis purpureis'

15 *Rosmarinus officinalis*
16 *Amaranthus* (dark red)

ANNUAL

17 *Carthamus tinctorius* (orange)
18 *Craspedia globosa*
19 *Helichrysum bracteatum monstrosum*
20 *Linum usitatissium*
21 *Lonas inodora*
22 *Tagetes erecta* (orange/yellow)
23 *Moluccella laevis*
24 *Delphinium consolida* (white)
25 *Ammobium alatum*

GRASS

26 *Panicum miliaceum*

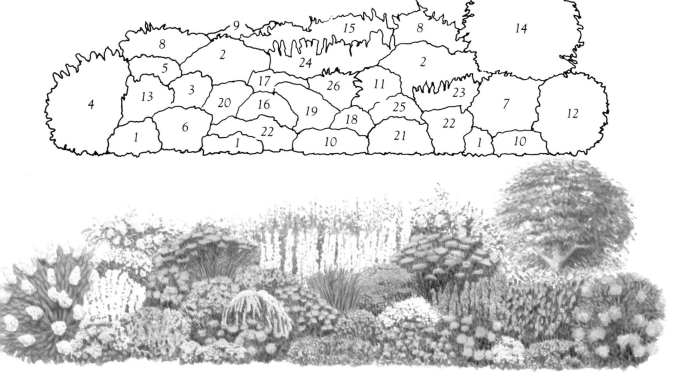

Blue, Cream, Grey, Purple and Silver

The cool, restful blues and greys of this scheme are given a touch of warmth by the flowers of the artichokes and honesty, and highlighted in summer by the soft yellow of the *Phlomis* and curry plant. *Ceonothus impressus* would make a lovely background to the scheme or, alternatively, *Eleagnus* x. *ebbingei* in exposed sites.

PERENNIAL

1 *Agastache mexicana*
2 *Acanthus mollis*
3 *Anaphalis margaritacea*
4 *Campanula glomerata*
5 *Delphinium elatum* (dark and pale blues)
6 *Echinops ritro*
7 *Eryngium planum*
8 *Eucalyptus gunnii* (pruned to form a shrub)
9 *Helichrysum angustifolium*
10 *Lavandula spica*
11 *Limonium latifolium*
12 *Lunaria biennis*
13 *Paeonia lactiflora* 'Duchesse de Nemours'
14 *Phlomis fruticosa*
15 *Rosmarinus officinalis*
16 *Rosa* sp. (rambler, double-flowered)
17 *Salvia officinalis* (and *Salvia officinalis* 'Tricolor')
18 *Senecio greyi*
19 *Hydrangea*
24 *Eleagnus* x. *ebbingei* (in exposed locations) or *Ceanothus impressus*
25 *Cynara cardunculus*

ANNUAL

20 *Papaver somniferum*
21 *Scabiosa stellata*
22 *Xeranthemum annuum*

GRASS

23 *Setaria italica*

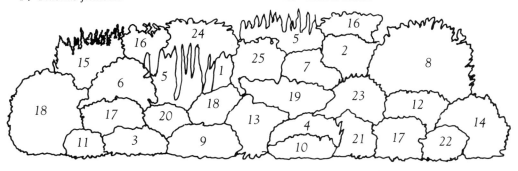

A dozen of the best

It is not always possible to give space to every plant you would like to grow and decisions always have to be made — which plant should you leave out and which ones must be given space at all costs? If you are short of space or spoilt for choice this scheme would provide a good basic collection of plants and plenty of versatile material (and could, if needed, be supplemented by commercially dried flowers). Once you have become proficient at growing and drying, your enthusiasm may well grow in proportion, making you determined to find more garden space for an ever-expanding collection.

PERENNIAL

1 *Hydrangea macrophylla* (pink/blue)
   Hydrangea paniculata 'Grandiflora' (white)
2 *Paeonia lactiflora* (cream, pink)
   Paeonia officinalis (red, cerise)
3 *Rose sp.* (rambler, double-flowered)
4 *Lavandula spica* (dark blue)
5 *Achillea ptarmica* 'The Pearl'
6 *Gypsophila paniculata*
7 *Limonium tartaricum dumosa*

ANNUAL

8 *Nigella damascena*
9 *Delphinium consolida* (white, pink, blue)
10 *Helichrysum bracteatum monstrosum* (mixed)
11 *Limonium sinuatum* (mixed)

GRASS

12 *Phalaris canariensis*

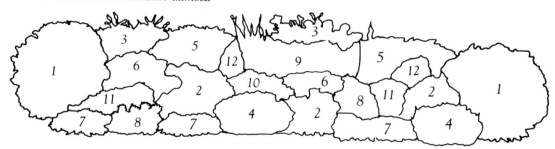

HARVESTING
AND DRYING

Harvesting should take place at the correct time for the plant in question (see the A–Z section). Timing the picking is very important for top-quality results — it is critical to within hours when drying peonies, within a day for *Helichrysum*, within a day or two for *Carthamus* and within a few days for grasses. There are also other problems to beset you, such as a sudden shower of rain just when you had planned to pick something, that may ruin the petal colour of your crop. However, taking care to pick at the best moment will prevent petal drop and keep the colours at their peak. All plant material should be picked on a dry day after any dew has evaporated. The stalks should be cut cleanly with secateurs or a sharp knife and medium-thick rubber bands used to hold the stems together. If a plant has woody stems that are unlikely to shrink then raffia or string can be used to tie them up. Any leaves around the base should be stripped off and the rubber band placed near the base of the stalk so the flower heads are not crushed together. The stems shrink considerably during drying so the bands need to be tight initially. Bunches should be kept small to help the drying process, especially if the drying conditions are slow or the stems very thick or fleshy.

Drying techniques

There are several ways to preserve the material you have painstakingly grown and picked, and the method used will depend on the particular plant with which you are working and your own resources. The A–Z section concentrates on plants which can be successfully air-dried, but there is also an appendix at the back of the book listing additional items which are suitable for glycerining and drying by the silica gel method.

Air-drying is by far the easiest and cheapest method of preserving plants. It produces material that can be fragile, but which, if handled with care, easily makes up into large and impressive displays in fireplaces or into delicate arrangements in small containers such as tea cups.

Glycerining produces robust and pliable material that can be handled many times and, indeed, can be wiped with a damp cloth should it become dusty. However, the process itself does not always have a 100 per cent success rate and often causes colour loss, so beginners may find it safer to start with air-drying and become proficient in this before progressing on to the glycerine treatment.

Silica gel is the third preserving method discussed in this book and produces a very different effect. The flowers are large and perfect, in fact some look good enough to be fresh, but they are extremely brittle and have to be dried on wired stems, so this method is not as useful for those who wish to make large arrangements. However, if miniature arranging is more appealing to you then drying with silica gel may be the answer. It certainly produces a superior result to air-drying, as can be seen on p. 38. However, this method takes up a lot of time and space and it may not be possible to produce the quantity of dried material that you would like.

AIR-DRYING

Providing a few basic rules are followed with air-drying, it is a very straightforward method of preserving flowers and you should achieve a very high success rate. Before picking anything it is important to decide where your drying area is going to be. The worst possible locations are by windows or in a greenhouse or garden shed because dampness and sunlight will spoil the colours. Ideally you should choose somewhere dry, dark and well-ventilated, with heat available. The perfect place would be a capacious boiler cupboard or an empty airing cupboard. Other possibilities include a spot over or near hot water pipes or over radiators and, if you happen to have an Aga cooker or something similar, then bunches hanging over and near it not only look decorative but also dry beautifully. In all cases the bunches should be hung away from any steam or damp air, both of which will defeat the object of the exercise, and they should never be left in places where they might constitute a fire hazard. They can be suspended on hooks, canes or lengths of strong wire. You can buy a reproduction of an old-fashioned laundry airer which can be pulleyed up and down from the ceiling, and this would make an excellent area for drying or storing dried flowers, assuming the room is not too light and sunny.

Heat is not always essential, but in many cases it can spell the difference between a resounding success and a rather mediocre result. If you have room in an airing cupboard and wish to raise the temperature a little, the lagging can be temporarily removed from the tank. Should you be lucky enough to live in a hot dry climate then heat may not be needed at all, but darkness and good ventilation will be important. The humidity of the drying area should be

watched, and if necessary, air circulation improved or a dehumidifier installed to speed up the process. Dehumidifiers are also invaluable during storage — it is surprising how fast dried flowers reabsorb atmospheric moisture.

The bunches should then be hung upside down in the dark as soon as possible. Ensure they are hanging completely vertical or they will dry crooked and bent. The rate of drying varies with each variety, bunch size, atmospheric conditions, temperature and so on, but it is important to be able to assess when the material is thoroughly dry. This is when the densest part of each flower head is dry and stems beneath the rubber band snap when bent. It is worthwhile destroying a few specimens in order to confirm that they are completely dry, otherwise mould or general deterioration will appear later.

There are several varieties which dry very happily standing upright. Many of the plants picked at the seed pod or seed head stage, such as Chinese lanterns, come into this category, but it also applies to sturdy stemmed items such as artichokes and gypsophila, some foliage and, of course, hydrangeas. For exact details and drying instructions, please refer to the details under the relevant heading of the A–Z section, beginning on p. 45.

USING SILICA AND OTHER DRYING AGENTS

An alternative method to air-drying is to use a desiccant — sand, borax or silica gel crystals. The end results are sometimes quite stunning and it is certainly worth experimenting with this method to see if it appeals to you or not. To work successfully with silica or other drying agents you must be patient and have very nimble fingers, because the dried material can be extremely brittle and therefore easily damaged.

Without doubt, the best desiccant to use is silica gel crystals, as the other possibilities such as sand and borax can be too coarse and leave marks on the flower petals. Silica gel is, however, fairly expensive but with careful use can last for many years and be reused endlessly. Many brands of silica gel crystals are sold in a plastic container, making them very convenient to use. If you purchase some without such a container then either use a half-gallon ice cream container or an old biscuit tin.

Bearing in mind the higher cost of this method of drying, there seems no point in drying plants in this way when you have perfectly satisfactory results with air-drying. Instead, concentrate on such plants as lilies, freesias, single

A warm spot in the kitchen, away from steam or moisture, can be ideal for drying bunches of flowers.

roses, garden roses and other flowers which can look significantly better with this method. (See Appendix VI for flowers that are suggested as suitable for this treatment.)

First check that your crystals are completely dry. In many cases they are sold with an in-built colour indicator, and are a strong blue colour when completely dry. Once they start to absorb moisture they gradually turn pink. If the crystals need drying, spread them on a shallow oven tray and place in the oven on a medium to low heat for about 45 minutes.

Using silica gel crystals

Any flowers you are planning to dry in this way should be as fresh as possible, so do not waste space on blemished or eaten specimens. Stalks or stems do not dry well with desiccants and so need to be trimmed to about 1 in (2.5 cm) long or less. Ideally, flowers should be wired while they are fresh, as this is far easier than trying to insert wires in brittle desiccant-dried material. A short stub wire can be pushed up the stalk while the flower is fresh, and then the required length of wire can be added once the drying has taken place.

Silica gel can produce very dramatic results, as shown by these 'Handel' roses.

The equipment you will need is as follows:
A plastic or tin container of silica gel crystals
A second container of approximately the same size
A child's small paintbrush
A teaspoon

First place a bed of crystals approximately 1 in (2.5 cm) deep in the empty container and then position the flowers so that they rest on the crystals but do not touch each other. Then carefully spoon in more crystals beneath, around and inside each flower, taking care to maintain the basic shape and support the flower heads. Once the flowers are completely buried, replace the lid of the container and store in a warm place (if possible) for approximately 48 hours. Some materials, such as daisies and smaller items, may take a little less time, and some slightly longer.

Check the flowers as soon as possible after the 48 hours have elapsed, as material left in the desiccant for too long can become over-brittle and fall to pieces. Take great care when unearthing the flowers as they will be very fragile — it is best done with the paintbrush, very gently. Any sudden gouging with the spoon or any other weapon may well cause irrepairable damage. Once you have gently extricated the flower check to see if it is completely dry or whether it requires a little longer, in which case the process must be repeated but this time leaving the flower for 24 hours instead of 48.

Having ascertained that the flowers are completely dry you should apply a light coat of matt varnish to prevent any reabsorption of moisture. Many varieties can manage well without this but a beginner would do better to assume that most varieties will reabsorb moisture and then to gradually experiment with and without varnish.

The finished flowers must be stored in an airtight container and, as a precaution, it is wise to add a small amount of silica gel crystals to the base of the container to keep any moisture to a minimum. Stems can then be lengthened with wires to fit into the desired arrangement. An ideal way to use desiccant-dried material is to display it under a glass dome, which shows off the beauty of the flowers but offers protection to their fragile condition.

GLYCERINING

Another method of preserving plant material is to replace the plant's own moisture with a glycerine and water solution. Although this is a rather unpredictable method of preserving plants, it is worth mastering for the unusual items that you can add to your collection that cannot be preserved in any other way.

It is essential to harvest material intended for glycerine treatment when it is fully mature, as glycerine is not happily absorbed by either immature or over-ripe plants. New growth does not accept the glycerine at all, so no matter how wonderful a bright green new shoot looks, don't try to pick it as it will only go limp and fail. Mid-season is the best time to pick anything destined for the glycerine treatment as it will be well matured but not past its best.

Suitable plants

There are many plants mentioned in the main A–Z section as being suitable for glycerine treatment, but the most successful are both deciduous and evergreen foliage. The leaves shown in the photograph are *Choisya* and *Helleborus corsicus* and *H. foetidus*. Many others are popular choices, such as beech, holly, ivy, laurel and magnolia, but it's fascinating to experiment and find something unusual that comes out well.

The process is fairly straightforward. Make a mixture of approximately 50 per cent boiling water and 50 per cent glycerine and pour it into a fairly tall narrow container. The ends of woody stems should be well battered with a hammer to help absorption. Stand the foliage in the mixture so that at least 3–4 in (7.5–10 cm) of each stem is below the surface. Then leave the plant material and glycerine mixture in a dark place and wait for the absorption to take place. It usually happens after about a week but some things take longer, and many items take two or even three weeks. You can tell when the leaves are ready as there will be some colour change and the leaves will feel smooth and pliable.

If small beads of glycerine appear on the surface of a leaf then remove that piece of foliage from the solution immediately. Dry off the beads of glycerine with a tissue and store in an even temperature away from strong light. It's interesting to treat the same type of foliage in two jars, placing one in sunlight and the other in darkness. Generally, one gets better colour by glycerining in the dark but a paler colour can make a lovely contrast and add to the interest of the arrangement.

One of the joys of glycerined material is that it gives you some leaves to work with, as most do not air-dry and therefore you can be left with a definite preponderance of flowers and very little foliage. This is especially so when you're trying to make a larger arrangement, as then leaves are very effective for both bulk and shape.

It is also useful to glycerine individual leaves as they can be used in smaller work. In this case, it is easier to use a shallow container and immerse the entire leaf in the glycerine solution. Again the mixture should be equal measures of glycerine and water and the process will take about the same length of time, sometimes a little less.

Whether working with large or small foliage, don't let the level of the glycerine and water mixture drop too low or dry out during the treatment but keep topping it up to the recommended depth, and don't discard the left-over liquid after you remove the plant material, as it can be reused next time.

Glycerine is very useful for preserving foliages that do not dry well by the air-drying method.

Using antifreeze

Another alternative to glycerine is to use car antifreeze. The main objection to glycerine is usually its cost, and antifreeze is considerably cheaper. Again, it is best to mix equal quantities of antifreeze and boiling water. Although this method is less expensive, experience has proved that better results have been achieved more consistently with glycerine, and some plants don't seem willing to absorb the antifreeze at all. Having said that, other foliage takes up the antifreeze and not glycerine so, again, experiment with pieces from the garden. I haven't found any problems with the blue colouring of antifreeze coming through into the foliage but some people say the colour has dyed their plant material a light blue shade, so do bear this in mind.

While we are on the subject of colouring and dyes, it is very easy to alter or just boost the colour of your material you are treating by adding a water-based dye to the original mixture. Sometimes natural material can be dyed subtly, and one should aim at enhancing the natural colour rather than creating a totally new false colour.

Storing dried material

Once you have gathered your plants and dried them successfully, your enthusiasm may lead you to drying many more bunches than you can use immediately. Much drying obviously takes place in the summer months, and the resulting material may well not be used until later in the year. Having spent a lot of time and effort on the drying technique, it is extremely important to store material carefully so that no deterioration occurs before you use it.

If you are using a dark dry area to dry flowers and you have unlimited space, then the bunches can just be stored where they were dried. Most people, however, are constantly short of drying space and need to clear it as soon as possible to make room for more pickings! If this is the case then sturdy cardboard boxes are probably the answer. The majority of florists are only too happy to let you have a couple of flower boxes in which they collected their stock from market that morning, and the shape and size of these boxes is ideal.

Ensure that the box is completely dry and has no holes in it — even the carrying holes on each end of some boxes should be sealed over as they make excellent doorways for insects or mice! Lay the bunches carefully in the box, making sure you don't bend any delicate stems against the end of the box. Once you have laid a layer of, say, five bunches at one end of the box, cover with tissue paper as shown in the photograph. Another layer can then be laid over the original one. Take care never to store material dried in different ways in the same box, e.g. keep air-dried and glycerined material apart, and glycerined material separate from silica-dried flowers.

It is recommended that you seal the boxes well as that will help minimize insect damage and also entry by any members of the rodent family. Boxes of dried material not only provide very edible seed heads but also beautifully colour co-ordinated mouse bedding! The boxes should be stored in a dry place, free of mice. Some lofts may be ideal, but not if they are uninsulated as some dampness may well be present. This also applies to garages and sheds.

Insect damage

If you should come across bunches where petals are disintegrating on to the floor, or where the base of the petals is being eaten away, then this is very likely to be caused by insect damage. Throw away any bunches that are badly damaged. If, however, the damage is only slight at that point, or if you want to play safe, place the bunch in the deep freeze for 24–48 hours and then hang up to dry again. This treatment seems to effectively eradicate any insect problems.

It seems obvious, but efficient labelling can save many minutes of frenzied hunting through boxes for a certain bunch you are trying to locate. It is useful to mark each box with a date as well as a list of its contents so the dried material can be used in rotation.

Flowers should be carefully stored between layers of tissue paper in a warm, dry place.

The A–Z of Recommended Plants

Introduction

This A–Z section includes a wide range of flowers which can be dried. It is by no means an exhaustive list — there are many other flowers, foliage and seeds worthy of experimentation!

Some of the plants listed are ideal for beginners — easy to grow and virtually dry by the time they are harvested. Others are more difficult and have specific requirements for harvesting and drying. Many of the flowers are familiar to gardeners, but the list also includes grasses and cereal crops which dried flower arrangers frequently use and may, therefore, consider to be worthwhile growing in small plots.

The growing hints should be referred to as general introductory guidelines and more detailed cultural advice sought where necessary.

The harvesting and drying recommendations should be read in conjunction with the relevant chapter in this book and it is to be assumed, unless otherwise stated, that flowers should be placed in the dark and the drying process started as soon as possible after cutting.

Papaver somniferum

ACACIA decurrens dealbata

MIMOSA

Deciduous Shrub

Mimosa bears clusters of small, round, yellow flowers which are strongly fragrant. The fern-like leaves are light green and feathery.

GROWING HINTS

Being frost tender, mimosa should only be established as a wall plant in warm locations. It will not grow well on lime.

HARVESTING AND DRYING

The flowers are produced from late winter into early spring. Cut when in full flower. Do not strip the leaves as they are also attractive to use. Air-dry hanging upside down.

ACANTHUS mollis

A. spinosus

BEAR'S BREECHES

Deciduous Perennial

Acanthus is a dramatic perennial, useful in the garden for its large, glossy, green ornamental leaves which inspired decorative patterns used in Greek Corinthian architecture. In summer it produces a 4–5 ft (1.2–1.5 m) tall distinctive white and purple flower spike which can be easily dried for use in large, extravagant arrangements.

GROWING HINTS

Acanthus can be grown from seed, but since only a few may be required to give an effect in the garden, it is probably best purchased as a small plant which will flower the following summer. It will grow in full shade but flowers best in full sun. The flowers of Acanthus spinosus are equally effective, though shorter — 3–4 ft (1–1.2 m). Acanthus can become invasive.

HARVESTING AND DRYING

Harvest in late summer when as much of the spike as possible is in full flower, but before the colour fades. Although sturdy it is best hung upside down to dry to prevent the tip bending over. Make sure the thick stems are fully dry before storage or use.

ACHILLEA filipendulina

var. 'Gold Plate' and others

YARROW

Deciduous Perennial

This is a popular and familiar plant of herbaceous borders, easy to dry and sturdy to use. The distinctive flat-topped yellow heads, measuring 3–4 in (7.5–10 cm) across, are formed on strong erect stems 3–4 ft (1–1.2 m) long. They are invaluable in indoor arrangements of all but the smallest size and look especially good with green millet or wheat, the warm orange of Helichrysum and Carthamus and clear bright yellow statice.

GROWING HINTS

Achillea filipendulina is tolerant of most soil types but enjoys full sun. It will eventually form a large clump, and the bright yellow flowers stand out best against a background of dark green or purple foliage. Tall varieties need staking or other forms of support.

HARVESTING AND DRYING

The exact timing of harvest in late summer is not very critical but, ideally, the stems should be cut when the individual florets are fully open and the flower head as a whole feels firm to the touch. The bunches will air-dry easily.

When drying or storing the bunches, make sure the heads are not crushed together as their shape is all-important. Do not, however, discard good flowers formed on bent or twisted stems as these can be used to artistic effect!

ACHILLEA *millefolium*

var. 'Cerise Queen' and others

YARROW

Deciduous Perennial

The common white yarrow is frequently found on road verges but, for the garden, several pink and pastel-coloured varieties

Achillea millefolium 'Summer Pastels'

are now available. Because of its soft colouring its use in dried arrangements tends to be as a filler or background shade to offset other bright flowers. For instance, the 'Cerise Queen' variety works well with pink *Helichrysum*, roses or peonies.

It may be worthwhile selecting strong-coloured varieties for planting since the colours tend to change during drying — for instance, from cerise to more dusky shades of plum. It can be used in arrangements of all sizes.

GROWING HINTS

Achillea millefolium is tolerant of most soils and prefers full sun. If sown in late spring it will flower the following year in summer. Though similar in form to *A. filipendulina*, it is shorter, flowering on stems 2–2½ ft (60–75 cm) high, so needs to be nearer the front of the border. The stems also tend to be weaker, so some support may be necessary at flowering time.

HARVESTING AND DRYING

Harvest in late summer, waiting until the flowers are in full colour. The small stems within the flower head need time to strengthen and firm up — if picked too early they remain limp and make the flower less strong for dried use.

The branches should be air-dried, hanging upside down. They must be fully dry before use.

ACHILLEA *ptarmica*

var. 'The Pearl'

SNEEZEWORT

Deciduous Perennial

'The Pearl' is a popular and easily-grown plant of great value to gardeners and flower arrangers. The small white double flowers are borne in profusion on long, 2–3 ft (60–100 cm), stems throughout the summer. 'The Pearl' is useful with any garden colour schemes and in arrangements provides a good highlight to offset other colours. It can be used in small-scale arrangements, but its long stems make it valuable when grouped in combination with taller flowers, especially larkspur and peonies. It is a good all-rounder.

GROWING HINTS

It is important to select a consistent double-flowering variety. Sow in late spring to flower the following year. *A. ptarmica* spreads rapidly so needs to be given space in the middle or back of the border. It likes sun or partial shade. Treatment for mildew on the leaves may be necessary during the summer. Dead stems should be cut back to ground level in the autumn.

HARVESTING AND DRYING

Cut when the flowers are well open but before the oldest flowers on the stem start to show signs of browning. Rain can easily damage the quality of the flowers so, if necessary, cut back poor quality stems and wait for a second flush of flowers to appear.

Hang the bunches upside down. It is important that the whiteness of the flowers is retained. Drying too fast at a high temperature can cause browning of the petals, while drying too slowly may result in colour loss on the stems and leaves and give a less fresh appearance. Ideally *Achillea* should be dried in a warm current of air.

ACROCLINIUM *roseum*

SUNRAY

Annual

One of the traditional everlasting flowers, *Acroclinium* is an annual with daisy-like flowers on fine stems. A range of colours is available — white, pinks and reds with yellow or black centres — all of which hold their colour well during drying. They can be used singly in small arrangements or bunched in mass as strong focal points in others.

GROWING HINTS

Sow under glass in early spring or outdoors in late spring, to flower in the summer. Use as a front of border plant or in locations where space is limited.

HARVESTING AND DRYING

Harvest before the flowers are completely open as they will develop further during drying. Hang the bunches upside down. *Acroclinium* air-dries easily.

AGASTACHE *mexicana*

A. urticifolia alba

AGASTACHE

Deciduous Perennial

Agastache looks very similar to mint, with 2–3 ft (60–100 cm) long spikes of either blue (A. *mexicana*) or white (A. *urticifolia alba*) flowers and nettle-like leaves. The plants have aromatic leaves, smelling of mint or lemon. The blue variety is useful as a background to bright pinks. The white flowers, however, become less significant when dried, leaving a light green spike particularly effective in contrast to bright reds.

GROWING HINTS

Agastache is not a common garden variety, so the seed or plants may be difficult to obtain.

If sown in early spring, it should flower in late summer in its first year and in mid-summer in following years. It grows well in full sun and is attractive to bees. Cut back in autumn.

HARVESTING AND DRYING

Wait until it is fully in flower and the spikes are 2–3 in (5–7.5 cm) long. The stem needs to have time to firm up before cutting otherwise, once dried, it will tend to become limp if exposed to damp atmospheres. It is better to pick too late than too early. However, do not allow the white flowers to discolour to brown as this will impair the appearance after drying.

After the leading stems have been cut, lateral branches will develop, allowing a second harvest.

Strip unnecessary leaves from the base of the stems before drying. These can be dried separately for use in pot pourri. Hang upside down to air-dry but ensure the stems are fully dry before using in arrangements.

ALCHEMILLA *mollis*

LADY'S MANTLE

Deciduous Perennial

The mass of minute lime-green flowers produced in summer are useful when dried as a delicate filler in small basket arrangements. In the garden *Alchemilla* is equally valuable as an edging plant or for planting under dark green or purple leaved shrubs.

GROWING HINTS

If purchased as seed, it must be sown in the autumn to germinate in the spring. Once established it seeds freely and grows best in a moist soil.

HARVESTING AND DRYING

Timing of cutting is not too critical but it must be while the flower mass retains its fresh green appearance and has not begun to deteriorate to yellowish brown. Being such a small, delicate flower head it dries easily, and faster drying with warm air will help to maintain the fresh colour.

ALLIUM sp.

ONION, LEEK, CHIVE, ETC.

Bulb

Leaving the remains of the vegetable crop to go to seed can provide some useful additions to a collection of dried flowers but be warned — they never completely lose their smell!

The various ornamental onions available for the flower garden can be chosen to flower throughout the summer and most are pink, mauve or white. They range from small rockery varieties to the large A. *aflatunense* which can grow up to 5 ft (1.5 m) in height. Generally, those with denser flower heads will dry best, though the rather different, spear-shaped head of A. *siculum* is excellent for drying.

GROWING HINTS
Most of the onion family enjoy a sunny position and can spread freely if allowed to seed.

HARVESTING AND DRYING
The flowers can be cut as the buds start to open or left until the seed heads have developed. The stems are very fleshy and so it is best to band only two or three together, hang them upside down, and allow them a long time to dry. Drying too slowly can cause deterioration and discoloration of the stems, so choose a warm place where the smell will not give offence!

ALLIUM christophii

syn. A. albopilosum

CHRISTOPHII
Bulb

This distinctive variety deserves a special mention because of its dramatic seed head resembling an exploding firework, which can easily measure 7 in (17.5 cm) across.

GROWING HINTS
The flowering stems are short so the plant should be established near the front of the border or alongside a patio, where it can enjoy a sunny position. The flowers are mauve and complement white and pink colours in the garden. Seeds should be sown in the autumn but establishment is not reliable and propagation by division is more successful. Once established, *Allium christophii* spreads naturally.

HARVESTING AND DRYING
A. *christophii* flowers in late spring or summer and the flower heads can be left until they have dried on the plant. Cut with as long a stem as possible and store in an airy place, preferably by hanging or standing them individually to prevent damage.

ALNUS glutinosa

COMMON ALDER
Deciduous Tree

The common alder is a tree frequently found adjacent to water or in damp locations. The alder's main value to the dried flower arranger lies in its small cones which are popular for small arrangements such as wreaths and in Christmas decorations.

GROWING HINTS
The trees are cheap to buy, especially when small. The upright habit of the common alder and the larger Italian alder, *Alnus cordata* (which has bigger fruits), and their growth rate make them suitable for screen planting or shelter belts.

HARVESTING AND DRYING
The cones can be cut when green in late summer and dried slowly or left until the autumn when they have turned dark brown.

AMARANTHUS paniculatus

A. caudatus

LOVE-LIES-BLEEDING
Hardy Annual

Amaranthus caudatus is best known as 'Love-lies-bleeding' because of its long trailing crimson tassels, on stems which

Amaranthus paniculatus

can be 3–4 ft (1–1.2 m) tall. It can be dried and used to good effect, but it is the shorter growing form, A. *paniculatus*, that is more popular with dried flower arrangers. It has dense erect plumes in either light green or dark red. The latter are especially valuable in dried arrangements as a dense, rich background to light pink larkspur or *Helichrysum*.

Do not confuse either form with A. *tricolor*, which is a foliage pot plant.

GROWING HINTS

Sow in late spring to flower in mid to late summer. *Amaranthus* likes an open position and its erect form is best used in more formal garden schemes.

HARVESTING AND DRYING

Wait until the whole plant is in full flower and the yellow stamens have just started to appear. Pick the entire stalk and dry as a whole. The leaves can be removed later, if necessary, but can usefully be retained in view of the flower's value as a filler in arrangements. Side shoots will provide a second crop.

Dry A. *caudatus* upright to retain the trailing effect. Dry A. *paniculatus* upside down to retain the erect plumes. To prevent the flowers developing beyond their prime, dry at warm/hot temperatures. The stems can be quite dense so ensure they are fully dry before use.

AMBROSINIA *mexicana*

AMBROSINIA

Annual

Ambrosinia has a tall, delicate, finely-pointed green flower spike with a fragrance similar to lemon balm. 'Green Magic' is a good variety for drying, growing to about 2 ft (60 cm) tall.

GROWING HINTS

The seed may be difficult to obtain. Sow in late spring, in an open position, to flower in late summer.

HARVESTING AND DRYING

The harvesting time is not critical. Cut when mature and air-dry quickly to retain the best colour.

It is essential that Ambrosinia is thoroughly dried upside down before use and subsequently not exposed to a damp atmosphere otherwise the tips will become limp and curl over.

AMMOBIUM *alatum* 'Grandiflorum'

WINGED EVERLASTING FLOWER

Annual

Ammobium flowers are best described as being like tiny pure white *Helichrysum*, but with daisy-like yellow centres when fully open. They are most useful in small arrangements or wreaths, with clusters of the flowers wired together.

GROWING HINTS

A native to Australia, *Ammobium* thrives in light, dry soils. It can be rather thin and ragged in form, so is perhaps best grown in a separate plot. Sown in spring, it will flower successively through the summer if continuously cut, the small flowers appearing at the end of green, winged stems 1–2 ft (30–60 cm) high.

HARVESTING AND DRYING

Harvest the stems selectively, choosing flowers that are half open. They will develop further during drying and may then display their yellow centres. If harvested too late the yellow centres will discolour.

The winged stems shrink dramatically during drying. What looked like a large fresh bunch may be rather small and bedraggled when dried, so be sure to pick enough. The bunches must be hung upside down as soon as possible after cutting and dried reasonably quickly to hold the pure whiteness of the flowers.

The stems always remain weak and

will rapidly absorb moisture again, causing the flower heads to droop. *Ammobium* must therefore be kept in a constantly dry atmosphere and may, even then, need support for the flower heads.

ANAPHALIS *margaritacea*

A. *yedoensis*

PEARL EVERLASTING
Deciduous Perennial

This delightful grey foliage plant is very effective in summer with its clusters of everlasting white flowers. The individual flowers are similar to *Ammobium* — opening to show a yellow centre.

GROWING HINTS
Anaphalis is probably easiest to obtain as a small plant. It spreads to form a clump enjoying full sun and a well-drained soil. *A. yedoensis* will also grow successfully in dry shady places. Growing to about 18 in (45 cm) high, *Anaphalis* is an ideal plant for the front of the border.

HARVESTING AND DRYING
Anaphalis flowers in late summer. Allow the leaves to remain on the stem when cutting, and air-dry hanging or upright. If dried too slowly the flowers will mature and go to seed. This can look attractive but will be too delicate for successful use.

ANETHUM *graveolens*

DILL
Annual/Herb

Dill is a valuable herb to have in any garden. It can also be left to flower and the dried seed head will retain some of its distinctive scent. The heads are similar in form to the delicate wild umbellifers such as cow parsley, but with yellowy-green flowers.

Anethum graveolens

GROWING HINTS
Dill can be sown from spring to early summer and will flower about ten weeks later. It will survive in any soil but will not flourish if too dry.

HARVESTING AND DRYING
The head, with as long a stem as possible, can be harvested at the flowering or seed stage and should be hung upside down to dry.

AQUILEGIA *hybrida*

COLUMBINE or GRANNY'S BONNET
Deciduous Perennial

The delicate columbine is a true cottage garden plant — a reliable perennial available in a range of soft shades of cream, pinks and blues. It flowers in late spring on stems 2 ft (60 cm) high.

GROWING HINTS
Sow in open ground so that the plants form small groups in the herbaceous borders. Once established they will seed freely. *Aquilegia* will tolerate most soil types but prefers sun or light shade and not too dry a soil.

HARVESTING AND DRYING
The flowers can be air-dried but it is the seed heads which are most useful. Pick them in early summer, while they are still a fresh green, and stand upright to air-dry. (They can be hung upside down but will shed seeds!)

In arrangements with other seed heads, the bright green is a lovely contrast to the orange of *Physalis franchettii*, Chinese lanterns, and the grey of poppy heads.

ARMERIA *caespitosa*

A. maritima

THRIFT or SEA PINK
Evergreen Perennial

Armeria is a low-growing perennial, forming dense green cushions with bright pink flowers growing to 6–12 in (15–30 cm) tall. It is an ideal plant for the rockery, flourishing in a sunny, well-drained position.

The bright pink flowers, on short stalks, appear in late spring or early summer. They should be picked in full flower and hung upside down to air-dry.

Their size makes them useful in small dainty arrangements. The colour changes to mauve during drying.

ASTER sp.

ASTER
Annual

The annual asters, which can be grown from seed, are deservedly popular as late-flowering bedding or edging plants and as cut flowers. Some of the larger double-flowered varieties, such as 'Milady' and 'Duchess', can provide unusual and strong colours for dried flower arrangements, though it is difficult to dry them successfully without petal loss. Cut the flowers just before they are fully open and hang up to dry quickly.

ASTER *novae-belgii*

MICHELMAS DAISY
Deciduous Perennial

Michelmas daisies can vary in height from dwarf varieties of less than 12 in (30 cm) up to more than 5 ft (1.5 m) tall. Some of the *Aster novae-belgii* hybrids which have a more double flower can be successfully dried. The tall dark-rose, crimson or red colours are probably the most useful.

GROWING HINTS
The perennial asters prefer a sunny, open position which is not too dry. Flowering in late summer or autumn, they make a valuable contribution to any garden.

HARVESTING AND DRYING
Harvest when the flowers are fully open and dry quickly to prevent them maturing too far. The petals will shrivel and curl but an effect will be achieved by the overall mass of flowers.

ASTILBE *arendsii*
FALSE GOAT'S BEARD
Hardy Perennial

The *Astilbe arendsii* hybrids are plants growing to 2–3 ft (60–100 cm) high with delicate flowering plumes, in colours from creamy-white to pink and dark red. The dark-leaved varieties can be used to contrast with light green foliage plants near the front of a border. (The white flowered *Astilbe* is difficult to dry without discoloration.)

GROWING HINTS
Astilbes are generally available for purchase as plants. They prefer partial shade and need a soil that is deep and moist. They are probably most at home near water.

HARVESTING AND DRYING
Flowering is in summer and the stems should be cut when the plant is in full flower but before it reaches maturity. Hang the stems upside down. Astilbe will air-dry easily in a warm place, but it is advisable to dry the white varieties more quickly.

ASTRANTIA *major*
MASTERWORT
Deciduous Perennial

Astrantia is a very natural cottage garden plant and looks good in well-established, rambling, herbaceous borders. It has small pinkish-white umbelliferous flowers on branching stems, growing to 2 ft (60 cm) in height.

GROWING HINTS
The seeds need to be sown in autumn so that they can overwinter before germinating. *Astrantia* enjoys full sun or partial shade but needs a moist soil. Once established, its roots will spread easily and it can be propagated by division.

HARVESTING AND DRYING
Astrantia flowers in early summer. The flowers can be successfully harvested when fully open and hung to air-dry.

ATRIPLEX *hortensis*
ORACH
Hardy Annual

Related to the dock family, *Atriplex hortensis* 'Rubra' is a crimson-leaved form, fast growing and very attractive as a contrast in herbaceous borders. Its tall seeding spike can be used in dried arrangements in a similar way to the red *Amaranthus paniculatus*. The green variety is a lovely light fresh colour.

GROWING HINTS
Sow in spring in open ground and harvest in late summer. It grows 4–5 ft (1.2–1.5 m) high.

HARVESTING AND DRYING
Cutting should be when the round flat seed pods have fully developed in size. If left too late the seeds will drop when dried. Use the dark colours to add depth to pink arrangements, or contrast strongly with yellows and light greens.

AVENA *sativa*
OATS
Hardy Annual Grass

Oats are an agricultural cereal crop, cultivated for porridge, breakfast cereals and horse feed. They grow taller than other cereals, reaching 4–5 ft (1.2–1.5 m), with seeds borne on pendulous panicles. Oats, especially when harvested green, are very useful in dried flower arrangements. They are one of the cheaper grasses to buy but, for serious growers, could be worth cultivating in a small plot.

GROWING HINTS

Different varieties are available for autumn or spring sowing. Oats require full sun and grow on a range of soil types.

HARVESTING AND DRYING

The ears emerge in late spring or early summer. Cut soon after the ear has emerged fully from the stem but while it is still bright and green. Hang upside down in the dark and dry quickly in warm air, to retain the colour. Alternatively, oats can be left to ripen naturally to their full harvest colour before cutting. At this stage additional drying is only necessary if the branches are to be stored. Late harvested oats can be dried upright.

BERGENIA hybrids

BERGENIA

Evergreen Perennial

The low-growing bergenia with its large evergreen leaves is a useful plant for the front of the border. It provides interest throughout the year and its pink flowers are particularly welcome in the garden in early spring. The best varieties for drying are those with densely-clustered flowers.

GROWING HINTS

Best purchased as plants, bergenia will spread to form a dense ground cover in ordinary soil, in sun or shade.

HARVESTING AND DRYING

At a time of year when there is little else available for drying, bergenia can be cut in full flower. The fleshy stems, which may be rather short, dry quickly in warm air and the pink flowers change to a delicate mauve. Wired in clusters, these provide an unusual touch in natural arrangements of soft pinks, green and white.

BRIZA sp.

QUAKING GRASS

Hardy Annual Grass

Quaking grass is a native of chalk grassland and is so named because of its delicate nodding seed heads, which remain long into the autumn. It has always been a popular ornamental grass and is best used in small, dainty arrangements.

GROWING HINTS

Quaking grass does not have the vigour to compete with other grasses in rich soils but will survive well on poor dry soils of low fertility, in full sun. The largest form, *Briza maxima*, will give the best effect but *B. media* and *B. minima* can also be used. Sow in spring, either in patches in the border or in plots or rows in a corner of the vegetable garden.

HARVESTING AND DRYING

Ideally, harvest in summer when the heads have developed fully but before the seeds are mature. However, timing is not critical and *Briza* can be harvested later although the colour will have faded. This grass will air-dry easily and quickly standing upright or hanging.

BROMUS sp.

B. macrostachys
B. secalinus

RYE BROME GRASS

Annual Grass

Many types of brome grass exist but *Bromus macrostachys* is worth mentioning as a distinctive full-headed variety. It is a light green grass, growing up to 2½ ft (75 cm) tall, with an open panicle form. The individual spikelets or seeds may develop a slight purple coloration with maturity. The fullness of its form makes rye brome a useful arrangement filler.

GROWING HINTS

Sow in the spring. Rye brome grows readily from seed and will thrive in poorer, drier soils in the open. It will survive mild winters and will self-seed readily. Sow in wild corners of the garden or restrict to plots.

HARVESTING AND DRYING

Wait until the branched panicle carrying all the seed heads has fully emerged from the stem. Cut while it is still green or wait (about a week) until the purple shades develop. Hang upside down. As with all grasses, the earlier the harvest and the faster the drying process, the greener the end product will remain.

CALLUNA *vulgaris*

ERICA sp.

HEATHER ('LING') or HEATHS

Evergreen Shrubs

The summer and autumn flowering heathers and the winter flowering heaths can be used as fillers in dried flower arrangements and should be cut in the early stages of flowering. They do, however, have a tendency to drop their leaves when dry, so are best used fresh and allowed to dry out *in situ* undisturbed. Alternatively, they can be sprayed with a fixative. A far superior result can be obtained using the glycerine method.

All prefer sandy, leafy, acidic soil and dislike lime.

CAMPANULA *glomerata*

CLUSTERED BELLFLOWER

Deciduous Perennial

Campanula glomerata gives reliable ground cover for the herbaceous border and, with its clusters of violet-blue flowers among bright green leaves, it provides, when dried, a natural-looking,

dark blue background filler for 'country' arrangements.

GROWING HINTS

Clustered bellflower spreads well in any soil that does not get too dry, in sun or partial shade. It flowers in early summer, on erect stems 1–2 ft (30–60 cm) high.

HARVESTING AND DRYING

The stems should be cut in full flower (but before the earliest clusters of blooms start to wither) and the leaves left on. Hang upside down to dry, fairly quickly, since retention of the green in the leaves is important.

CARLINA *acaulis caulescens*

CARLINE THISTLE

Deciduous Perennial

This is a very prickly plant to handle but well worth the effort! The carline thistle, fully mature with its silvery-white and biscuit-coloured seed heads, is an eye-catching specimen especially in autumnal arrangements.

GROWING HINTS

Sow in spring in an open sunny position on any soil. It is a stemless thistle flowering above a rosette of leaves and, once established, can tolerate dry conditions.

HARVESTING AND DRYING

The thistle flowers in summer, with heads 4–5 in (10–12.5 cm) across. Wait until the head has matured and is beginning to go to seed before harvesting.

Prolonged drying will be necessary because of the density of the head, so dry in a warm place and ensure the centre is thoroughly dry before using. The flower head will need to be wired or given a false stem before being used in arrangements.

CARTHAMUS *tinctorius*

SAFFLOWER

Annual

Until recently *Carthamus* was little heard of but, commercially, is now widely grown because of its usefulness as a dried flower. It bears distinctive, thistle-like flowers on tall, strong branching stems up to 3 ft (1 m) high. Like thistles, the leaves tend to be prickly although spineless varieties are now becoming available.

The orange varieties are very striking and lovely to use in combination with the yellow *Achillea filipendulina*, linseed, wheat, millet and dark red *Helichrysum*. A cream variety is less showy, but more versatile in colour combinations.

The strength and height of *Carthamus* are assets in tall arrangements but the individual heads can also be used in small arrangements — especially if picked in the green, unopened bud stage.

The green of dried *Carthamus* is particularly prone to fading in direct sunlight.

GROWING HINTS
Sow in spring in open ground. It will benefit from a good soil and grow tall and strong, though may need treatment for blackfly.

HARVESTING AND DRYING
Carthamus flowers in mid-summer. If the green bud stage is required, allow the buds to swell fully and cut as late as possible before they burst. If harvested too early the buds will shrivel when dried.

When planning to harvest *Carthamus* in full flower, careful observation is necessary. The terminal bud (not necessarily the tallest) will open first and then the secondary flowers will follow — slowly if the weather is cold and wet, but quickly if it is hot and dry. The first

Carthamus tinctorius

flower will begin to die off. The best quality will be achieved by cutting the stem when the maximum number of flowers are fully open, but before more than one or two have over-matured. (A certain proportion will still, inevitably, be in the green bud stage.) The leaves lower down the stem should still be fresh green at this harvesting stage. Rapid air-drying in the dark is necessary as the fresh greenness is an important characteristic of the plant. To check dryness, make sure the stems snap when bent and dissect a large flower head.

CELOSIA *argentea cristata*

COCKSCOMB

Half-hardy Annual

Cockscomb is best known as a pot plant with its unusually formed bright red flower. It is not commonly seen as a dried flower but the dense, dark red head can be useful to give depth of colour to arrangements with bright greens, warm oranges and yellows.

GROWING HINTS
Celosia is usually raised in greenhouse conditions, sown in early spring and transplanted four to five weeks later. Direct sowing is, however, possible in sheltered locations.

HARVESTING AND DRYING
Harvest when in full flower and do not strip the leaves. Hang upside down and dry rapidly to maintain the best colour. Snap the stems to test dryness.

CENTAUREA *cyanus*

CORNFLOWER

Half-hardy Annual

Cornflower is available in blue, pink, mauve, purple and white but it is the blue variety which is most sought after in dried flower arrangements. It is especially useful in small decorative work such as posies or arrangements around straw hats. It can look particularly appropriate in natural combination with wheat and grasses, for instance, plaited into the ties around wheatsheaves.

GROWING HINTS

Select strong growing double-flowered varieties with good stems. Sow in full sun in spring. To produce straight upright stems the plants need support so are best grown in rows or clumps. The flowers start to bloom about 12–14 weeks after sowing.

HARVESTING AND DRYING

Regular daily cropping is necessary to obtain the best quality flowers. Select only the flowers that have *just* opened fully. If allowed to mature further, the flowers will start to fade and be prone to petal drop after drying — pick these separately for use in pot pourri. Secondary buds will continue to develop so the flowers can be cropped over several weeks.

The weakest point in the stem is just below the head, so it is imperative that the flowers are not allowed to droop, but are hung upside down immediately. Rapid drying is essential.

CENTAUREA *macrocephala*

KNAPWEED

Deciduous Perennial

Centaurea macrocephala has large golden-yellow thistle-like flowers and bright green leaves. The stems are strong and can grow to about 3 ft (1 m) high. It is a very striking herbaceous plant or dried flower, especially if used in combination with other yellows, oranges and reds and against dark green or purple backgrounds. The brown, cup-shaped remains of the seed heads are also attractive in the autumn and useful as strong focal points.

GROWING HINTS

Sow in patches in late spring in an open position. It will survive but not grow tall if in too dry a location.

HARVESTING AND DRYING

Centaurea flowers in late summer. Wait until the yellow petals have burst through from the bud stage but do not allow the plant to flower fully before cutting — it will open further during drying. Dry rapidly to retain a good colour. The centre of the flower head will be the last part to dry fully.

Once the primary flowers have been cropped, side shoots will develop so extending the harvesting period over several weeks. These later flowers will have shorter stems that may need to be extended by wiring.

If left until the autumn to go to seed fully, what will remain is a brown 'cup' made up of small feathery sepals. These will need little further drying before they can be used but some of the old seeds may have to be removed if the heads are to look their best.

Spray gold or silver for Christmas arrangements.

CHRYSANTHEMUM sp.

CHRYSANTHEMUM

Hardy Perennial

Of the numerous chrysanthemum hybrids, those with dense, double-flowering heads dry best and some subtle colours can be obtained. They should be cut just before the flowers reach maturity and dried quickly to prevent the petals dropping. The petals shrivel during drying so the head size shrinks considerably.

The flowers are rarely suitable as focal points but make adequate additions to a colour scheme. Dark purple spray chrysanthemums are especially useful to give depth of colour to tall arrangements.

Centaurea cyanus

CLEMATIS sp.

CLEMATIS

Deciduous Perennial Climber

The clematis plants — including the common *Clematis vitalba* (Old Man's Beard) provide a source of decorative fluffy seed heads in the later summer and autumn. The stems can also be used as the basis for wreaths. The yellow flowering *C. tangutica* and *C. orientalis* can be particularly recommended.

GROWING HINTS

Clematis likes its roots to be in the shade, where the soil does not dry out too much, but the growing shoots to be in the sun. This makes it an ideal plant to use as a climber through other shrubs and trees. It benefits from periodic thinning out or pruning in spring. Specific cultural details should be noted for individual varieties.

HARVESTING AND DRYING

The harvesting stage of the seed heads is not critical, though quality may be damaged by wet weather later in the year. Once cut, they can be left to air-dry naturally. Later, the plants' stems can be cut back, trimmed and wound into circlets or heart shapes while still supple. They can be decorated immediately or left to dry out for later use as the basis for wall displays or table centres.

CORTADERIA *selloana*

PAMPAS GRASS

Perennial Grass

The giant plumes of pampas grass, rising out of large clumps of reed-like leaves, are unmistakable in any garden. Indoors they should only be used in large-scale arrangements.

GROWING HINTS

Pampas grass requires lots of space and a deep, good soil in a sunny position.

HARVESTING AND DRYING

The flowering heads appear in late summer and remain well into the autumn. The cream or pinkish plumes should be harvested when they have emerged fully but before they become mature, otherwise during drying they will become too fluffy as the seeds develop. If picked at the right stage, they can be stood upright to air-dry naturally and need not be confined to the dark.

CORYLUS *avellana contorta*

CORKSCREW HAZEL

Deciduous Shrub

This deciduous shrub or small, multi-stemmed tree is an ornamental addition to the garden because of its twisted branches and catkins in spring.

GROWING HINTS

The corkscrew hazel grows to about 10 ft (3 m) in height in all except very acid soils. Straight stems shooting from the base should be cut back each winter to favour the contorted ones.

HARVESTING AND DRYING

The branches are unusual enough to be used on their own or in very simple arrangements in vases or jugs. Select the most interesting shapes and cut when the branches are bare. They do not need to be dried before use. At Christmas they can be painted (with white, silver or gold) and hung with decorations.

Salix matsudana, the corkscrew willow, is a small fast-growing tree, easily rooted from cuttings. It also has twisted branches, though the contortions are less extreme.

COTINUS *coggygria* 'Foliis purpureis'

C. *coggygria* 'Royal Purple'

SMOKE TREE
Deciduous Shrub

The round dark purple leaves of these varieties of *Cotinus* are marvellous as background colouring in the garden and the fine feathery flowers on mature shrubs give the impression of smoke — hence the name. Both flowers and leaves can be dried, but it is the latter which will provide the most striking feature.

GROWING HINTS
Cotinus grows to about 10 ft (3 m) tall and thrives in any soil. It can feature as a specimen or be at the back of the border but will not look its best in shade. Place it in contrast to silver or bright green foliage plants or as a background to yellows (such as *Achillea filipendulina*), warm oranges or bright, light blues. The flowers are produced more profusely on mature and unpruned or lightly pruned plants.

HARVESTING AND DRYING
Pick the flowers in late summer and hang to air-dry. The leaves too should be left until late summer and can be pressed, dried slowly like eucalyptus or glycerined.

CRASPEDIA *globosa*

DRUMSTICK
Annual

The tiny yellow flowers of *Craspedia* are packed in a tight ball on the end of a long, clean, strong stem, thus resembling a drumstick. They last well as cut flowers and are also popular dried, forming a strong focal point in arrangements. Their distinctive shape is well illustrated in the display of garden flowers on page 19.

GROWING HINTS
The seeds should be sown early in spring under glass, pricked out four to six weeks later and planted out in late spring. *Craspedia* grows up to 3 ft (1 m) in height and support may be needed to ensure good straight stems.

HARVESTING AND DRYING
Craspedia flowers from late summer into the autumn and should be picked just as (or just before) the flowers reach their prime. The stems will stand upright but should not be dried too slowly or the flowers will deteriorate.

Craspedia globosa

CUCURBITA *pepo*

GOURD

Half-hardy Annual Fruit

These ornamental (but inedible) fruits can be grown in green, yellow, white or orange combinations of colours. They provide interesting ornaments for the winter.

GROWING HINTS

Like pumpkins or marrows, gourds are rambling plants and best allocated to a corner of the vegetable plot. They like a sunny position in any soil. Sow in spring under glass and plant out in early summer.

HARVESTING AND DRYING

Harvest when the fruits have developed to full size, about 4 in (10 cm) in diameter, and are ripe. Allow them to dry naturally at room temperature over a period of several weeks and then apply varnish to retain the bright colours.

CYNARA *cardunculus*

CARDOON

Deciduous Half-hardy Perennial

The cardoon is similar to the artichoke but not edible! It is taller but has a smaller, more thistle-like head with mauve-purple flowers that retain their colour well during drying. It branches more freely but has similarly architectural grey-green foliage and is a very attractive garden plant.

Growing, harvesting and drying rules are the same as for artichokes.

CYNARA *scolymus*

GLOBE ARTICHOKE

Deciduous Half-hardy Perennial

If the gastronomic delights of artichokes are forgone they can develop into dra-

matic flowers and be picked at various stages of their development for different effects. The large, mauve flower heads are held on thick, sometimes branched, stems 3 ft (1 m) or more high above decorative silver grey leaves.

The outer bracts of the heads are a greeny-grey colour, often with a dark purple tinge. If cut when small and closed they can be used as solid elements in arrangements with, for instance, dark red hydrangeas, bright red roses, *Nigella* and cocksfoot grass. If left longer and dried, so that they are captured in full flower, a group of stems on their own in an earthenware pot make an eye-catching feature. If the flower matures further towards seeding the colour fades and eventually the centre turns to a pale biscuit colour, surrounded by silvery white.

GROWING HINTS

Artichokes need a good moist soil and will benefit from mulching. Sow direct into open ground in spring, spaced 2 ft (60 cm) or more apart. If established early, flowers will develop in the first autumn. Subsequently, flowering will begin in summer. Their attractive foliage makes them equally suitable for corners of the flower border or the vegetable garden. Not all plants will survive a hard winter but those that do will grow to a significant size — 5 ft (1.5 m) in height and spread, and the mature flowering heads can measure 6 in (15 cm) across.

To be enjoyed as a vegetable, the heads need to be picked much earlier than for drying — while the globe is still tightly closed and before the tips of the edible outer bracts have developed sharp spines.

HARVESTING AND DRYING

As indicated above, the artichokes can be cut at different stages. The young unopened artichokes can be selected at various sizes and cutting these early in

Cynara scolymus

the season will encourage further buds to develop.

Drying an artichoke, so that its full flowering glory is captured, is more difficult. The head contains a reserve of moisture and continues to mature while drying, and the rate of development will vary according to the speed of drying. Cutting when the mauve flower petals just start to appear in the centre of the head usually results in the flower drying in its prime.

If the artichokes are allowed to flower naturally on the plant, the tufted seeds will eventually develop. This is also a very attractive stage at which to cut and dry the heads. Any parts of the centre discoloured by rain or dead petals can be gently pulled out. (This can be a prickly job!)

Artichokes need a *very* long time to dry. They can be hung upside down, stood upright or laid down. They must be in as warm a location as possible, but not necessarily in the dark. To test for dryness push a skewer into the densest underpart of the head at the top of the stem. If still soft, leave it longer to dry and harden, otherwise mould will ultimately develop.

DACTYLIS glomerata
COCKSFOOT GRASS
Perennial Grass

Cocksfoot is a perennial grass, historically important agriculturally in pastures and meadows and often found on road verges. Because it is indigenous and exists naturally in many larger gardens it is probably not worthy of special cultivation. However, it is valuable for use in 'natural' arrangements. The head is a dark, dull, green but with a purple tinge which makes it an ideal complement to flowering artichokes and red hydrangeas.

GROWING HINTS
Sown in late summer, cocksfoot will flower the following year in late spring. In its leaf stage cocksfoot is short, but in fertile sites the flowering stems can reach 4–5 ft (1.2–1.5 m) tall.

HARVESTING AND DRYING
Cut when the branched flower head, with its tightly packed spikelets (the individual flowers), has fully emerged. At first green, the purple coloration develops quickly after the head emerges. Harvest before the tiny yellow anthers can be seen hanging from the flower heads. Hang in bunches upside down and air-dry quickly to retain the colour. Ensure the parts of the stems under the rubber band are fully dry and brittle before storing.

DAHLIA sp.
DAHLIA
Half-hardy Annual (Tuberous)

The small double or pompom varieties of dahlia can be successfully air-dried and are available in a wide range of colours. (The richer colours are likely to be more successful.) They are by no means as spectacular when dried as they are fresh, but can nevertheless be useful for their colour and form.

GROWING HINTS
Dahlias grow easily from seed, cuttings or division of tubers. They can be planted out in any soil in a sunny position and will flower reliably in late summer. In a mild climate dahlias will overwinter.

HARVESTING AND DRYING
Pick in the early stages of full flowering and hang up to air-dry relatively quickly to prevent the flower overmaturing and losing petals.

DELPHINIUM *consolida*

LARKSPUR

Annual

Larkspur is indispensable as a dried flower and well worth growing in the garden. It is available in a variety of colours — pale and dark blues, pinks, mauves and white — and the flower

Delphinium consolida

spikes grow to about 3 ft (1 m) in height. It can be used in basket displays or arranged naturally, like a fresh flower, in a vase with grasses (such as *Setaria*), peonies and *Achillea ptarmica*.

GROWING HINTS
Select double-flowering types that have

large individual florets densely packed up the stem (*Delphinium ajocis* is not suitable). Sow in spring in any soil, in a sunny position. Do not transplant.

HARVESTING AND DRYING
As a fresh flower larkspur is usually cut when 50 per cent of the flowers are in bloom. Drying it at this stage retains the greenish buds at the tip of the stem and can give a fresh look to a display. However, larkspur is generally cut for drying when it is 90 per cent in flower. Cutting later than this or drying too slowly makes it susceptible to petal drop. It dries easily but should be dried fairly quickly hanging upside down.

A second crop of shorter stems may be obtained from side shoots after the leaders have been cut.

If storing in a box, make sure the tips are not bent against the box ends. However, if the blooms become crushed during storage, they can be opened out by holding the stems over steam for a short while.

DELPHINIUM *elatum*
DELPHINIUM
Deciduous Perennial

Though more difficult to dry successfully than larkspur, the tall hybrid delphiniums — growing up to 6 ft (2 m) tall — are useful for big arrangements. The large flowered and dark blue varieties can be particularly striking especially when used with bright greens and creamy whites. (The smaller *Delphinium belladonna*, with branched heads, is not so suitable for drying.)

GROWING HINTS
Plant in full sun, in the middle or back of the border, in rich, well drained soil. Take precautions against slugs which are attracted to the young shoots. The tall delphiniums are susceptible to wind damage, so provide support if necessary.

HARVESTING AND DRYING
Cut when the plant is 90 per cent in flower and air-dry fairly quickly, hanging upside down.

DIANTHUS *barbatus*
SWEET WILLIAM
Hardy Biennial

Sweet Williams are not an obvious choice for drying but they can provide a welcome splash of colour in the garden as well as being very useful background fillers to cover oasis in small arrangements. They are available in crimson, pink, white or variegated colours and should be grown at the front of herbaceous borders.

GROWING HINTS
Sow outdoors in late spring or early summer, thinning or transplanting as necessary. Flowers will appear in the late spring of the following year.

HARVESTING AND DRYING
Cut and bunch when in full flower and air-dry quickly. The petals will shrivel and become flecks of colour against the green or plum colouring of the bulk of the flower head. If the dried Sweet Williams are exposed to moisture in the air, they will rapidly deteriorate in quality. The greenness is also prone to rapid fading in bright sunlight.

DIANTHUS *caryophyllus*
D. x. *allwoodii*
CARNATION
PINK
Half-hardy Annual/Biennial
Hardy Perennial

The large double 'button-hole' type of carnation can be successfully dried. Though available in a range of colours, it is the strong reds which hold their colour best and can be most successfully used in dried arrangements.

The smaller perennial pinks also dry well and again it is the stronger darker colours which are to be recommended. The single flowers shrivel but the closed buds are decorative in small posy arrangements, though their greenness tends to fade rapidly in daylight.

GROWING HINTS
Carnations should be sown under glass in late winter or outdoors in late spring. They like a sunny position in fertile soil and will flower in late summer. Pinks are easily propagated from cuttings.

HARVESTING AND DRYING
Cut pinks and carnations when they are just in full flower and air-dry quickly, hanging upside down. The stems under the carnation heads may be weak and have to be wired.

DIPSACUS *fullonum*
COMMON TEASEL
Biennial

The common teasel has always been a favourite element in dried flower decorations, picked when it has turned brown in the autumn. But instead, try cutting it just as, or after, it bears its ring of mauve flowers and it will then retain its greenness when dried and thus look fresher and be more versatile in use.

Teasels are frequently found on road verges, stream banks and waste ground. Seeds can be collected in the autumn and if sown then will produce a large rosette of leaves in the first year, followed by tall flowering stems in the second.

Dipsacus fullonum

ECHINOPS *ritro*
GLOBE THISTLE
Deciduous Perennial

Globe thistles do not thrive in dry locations but, given the right combination of having their heads in the sun and their roots in moist soil, they will grow vigorously up to 6 ft (2 m) tall without needing food. The prickly grey leaves and steely-blue flower heads look good with delicate white and pale pink colourings or strong creams and fresh greens. The distinctive globe shape of the flowers, which grow up to 1½ in (3.5 cm) in diameter, give form and focus to arrangements, though they need careful handling as the heads will easily break off if knocked.

GROWING HINTS

Sow in late spring, to flower in late summer. Locate in the middle or back of a herbaceous border and allow plenty of space for each plant. The tall, rather soft stems may need support during the growing season.

HARVESTING AND DRYING

The cutting of globe thistles for drying needs careful timing. As the heads develop in size they change from grey-green towards lavender blue when the individual florets are about to break bud. The secret is to cut them at this stage before the florets open.

Hang upside down to air-dry. Once dry they need to be handled with great care — not only because they are very prickly but because the heads can be easily damaged or broken off.

If allowed to flower fully before cutting the dried heads will look untidy and be even more fragile.

ERICA sp.

HEATH

Evergreen Shrub

See *Calluna vulgaris*.

ERYNGIUM sp.

SEA HOLLY

Perennial

The sea hollies are all sturdy plants with silvery grey leaves and foliage and distinctive clusters of steely-blue flowers on branched stems. The biennial *E. giganteum* has large flower heads whereas the flowers of *E. alpinum* are smaller and bluer. They look good planted in borders with white or deep blues and purples but, being prickly, should not be too close to well-used paths!

Eryngium has very strong stems when dry. The tall branching stems of *E.*

planum (which may also be a pronounced blue in colour) can be used in big arrangements or the smaller heads arranged individually in posies. It is equally versatile with a range of colours — in combination with pink larkspur, dark blue lavender, cream *Helichrysum*, fresh green grasses or apricot statice.

GROWING HINTS

The seeds need to overwinter and germination can be slow but, once established, *Eryngium* likes full sun and will grow well in a dry, well drained soil or through gravel.

HARVESTING AND DRYING

The harvesting stage is not as critical as with *Echinops*. Wait until the flower heads have developed fully in size and start to turn blue. Air-dry hanging or standing.

EUCALYPTUS sp.

GUM TREE

Evergreen Tree

The silvery or grey-green leaves of eucalyptus are justifiably popular for fresh and dried flower arrangements. They are fast growing trees; many are frost tender but *E. gunnii*, the cider gum, is one of the hardiest. They are fairly tolerant of all soil types but, with the exception of *E. parvifolia*, dislike shallow chalk soils.

The foliage generally used by flower arrangers is the juvenile leaves, which can be distinctly different from those produced by the adult tree. However, eucalyptus responds well to hard pruning, which stimulates the continued production of juvenile leaves.

GROWING HINTS

If eucalyptus is being grown for its foliage rather than as a specimen tree it is best purchased as a small pot-grown tree and pruned to develop a shrub-like form.

HARVESTING AND DRYING

Eucalyptus can be used fresh in arrangements and allowed to dry in place naturally, or it can be bunched and hung upside down. It is important to dry eucalyptus slowly to prevent the leaves curling and becoming brittle and to hold the distinctive and attractive colour of grey-leaved varieties. Ideally, hang it somewhere in the house where its wonderful aroma can be enjoyed!

Eucalyptus can be preserved with glycerine. This process tends to turn the leaves a dark green.

EUPHORBIA polychroma

syn. E. epithymoides

CUSHION SPURGE
Perennial

Euphorbia polychroma spreads easily to form dark, green-leaved clumps. It flowers in spring, the flowers being insignificant but contained in bright yellow-green bracts on stems 18 in (45 cm) high. This fresh colouring stands out especially well against dark backgrounds and lasts a long time.

GROWING HINTS

Spurge can be propagated by cuttings, division or by seed sown in the autumn. The plants like sun or partial shade.

HARVESTING AND DRYING

The stems exude a milky sap which is poisonous and can be an irritant, so take care when cutting and handling. Harvest when the bracts have opened fully but before they start to lose their fresh colour. The cut ends of the stems can be sealed by placing them for a few seconds on a hot oven plate or in hot water. The bunches should then be hung upside down and dried slowly. Fast drying will cause shrivelling.

FAGUS sylvatica

F. sylvatica purpurea

BEECH
Deciduous Tree

It is a natural tendency of beech to hold much of its juvenile foliage during winter — a characteristic that makes it particularly valuable as a hedging plant. These dry light brown/bronze winter leaves can be used in their natural state or can be glycerined and dyed. The purple-leaved beech is particularly dramatic.

Beech mast — the seed pods — can be collected as they fall, or picked when closed, so that they open while drying. They are ideal for use in wreaths and Christmas decorations.

FESTUCA sp.

FESCUE GRASS
Perennial Grass

The fescues are a large family of grasses possessing very fine, delicate flowers on branched stems. Their fine form makes them suitable for delicate arrangements though, if cut in full flower, they are not to be recommended for use by hayfever sufferers! *Festuca ovina* (Sheep's fescue) is often included in lawn seed mixes and *F. glauca* (Blue fescue) forms clumps and is useful as a rockery or edging plant.

F. longifolia is one of the tallest species in this family, which generally have rather delicate seed heads. Fescues are tolerant of most soils and are drought-resistant.

GROWING HINTS

Sow in late summer, to flower in early summer the following year. Alternatively, simply allow selected areas of lawn grass to grow and flower, under trees for instance, and take a crop of whichever attractive species appear. With so many species and hybrids, it would need a skilled botanist to identify specimens which might be found naturally in larger gardens.

HARVESTING AND DRYING

Cut in the early stages of flowering, after the heads have emerged fully but before the anthers (and pollen) appear. Dry by hanging in warm air.

GOMPHRENA globosa

GLOBE AMARANTH

Half-hardy Annual

The globe amaranth is not a well-known garden plant but, like *Carthamus*, is becoming more widespread in popularity because of its everlasting qualities. It grows to 1 ft (30 cm) in height and has clover-like flowers in white, rose or purple. The latter is particularly distinctive. *G. haageana* has pastel orange flowers and is a little taller. All are useful in small arrangements both as fresh or dried flowers.

GROWING HINTS

Sow under glass in early spring and transplant out four to six weeks later. It flowers from early summer onwards and is a reliable plant for the front of the border.

HARVESTING AND DRYING

Cut when the flowers are completely open. They are naturally papery and will air-dry easily, hanging upside down.

GRAMINEAE sp.

GRASSES

Annual/Perennial Grasses

Grass species are numerous, varying in size and flower form. Certain types have attractive foliage so are suitable for inclusion in flower borders. Others are best grown in selected corners since it is only the flower head which is of interest

to the dried flower gardener. Select ornamental grass seed mixtures if establishing afresh, but don't forget the rougher corners and garden boundaries which will often yield a surprising variety of grass heads during spring and summer, without any establishment being necessary.

Specially seeded 'wild' garden areas have gained in popularity recently. Establishing wild flower, herb and grass gardens help to preserve native flora, as well as providing food for butterflies, bees and other insects. Choose seed mixtures with a good range of wild grass species if interested in harvesting for drying. The most important grasses for drying are listed separately in this A–Z (see Appendix III).

Listed below are other grasses which also dry well. Each will establish if sown in moist fine seed beds in spring, but many have minute seeds and will not tolerate very dry conditions until well-rooted. Harvest as soon as the flower heads have fully emerged to retain the freshest green colour. Hang upside down in a warm, airy, dark position. Most are fine-stemmed types, so dry easily.

ANNUAL

Agrostis nebulosa	Cloud grass
Aira elegans	Hair grass
Pennisetum villosum	Feathertop grass
Poa annua	Meadow grass
Polypogan monspeliensis	Beard grass

PERENNIAL

Deschampsia flexuosa	Wavy hair grass
Deschampsia caespitosa	Tufted hair grass
Pennisetum setaceum	Fountain grass
Stipa pennata	Feather grass

Hay fever sufferers are advised to cut grasses especially early and to be wary of working with grasses cut when in full flower, or which develop into full flower while drying.

GYPSOPHILA *paniculata*
var. 'Bristol Fairy'
BABY'S BREATH
Hardy Perennial

Gypsophila is a delightful flower to grace the garden and is invaluable in fresh and dried displays. A combination of dried roses and *Gypsophila* with green millet or *Agastache urticifolia* can be easily arranged in a vase as if they were fresh. *Gypsophila* is a wonderful filler for large arrangements, and a delicate and essential addition to any small wedding posies or head-dresses. For drying it is important to select a double-flowered variety which will give a frothy mass of tiny white flowers.

GROWING HINTS
Sow under grass in early spring and plant out into a sunny position in the middle of a border. *Gypsophila* prefers chalky, well-drained soils.

HARVESTING AND DRYING
Cut when it is in full flower. This is important as the flowers are so tiny and they need to be fully open to give the maximum effect. *Gypsophila* should be hung upside down with the bunches well separated from one another so they do not tangle. It will air-dry quickly and easily this way. Drying fast in heat will make the fine stems brittle and possibly discolour them. If storing in boxes, put tissue paper between the layers to prevent tangling and pack lightly to prevent crushing.

HELICHRYSUM *angustifolium*
syn. *H. italicum*
CURRY PLANT
Evergreen Shrub

The curry plant has narrow, silvery-green leaves that are strongly aromatic, and clusters of small yellow flowers in summer. Both flowers and foliage can be readily dried but the latter is probably most useful for texture and colour as a filler in arrangements.

GROWING HINTS
Whether in the herb or the herbaceous garden, the curry plant looks good in a front of border position in full sun. It likes a dry soil. It can be pruned to keep a neat rounded appearance, growing to about 1 ft (30 cm) high.

HARVESTING AND DRYING
The flowers should be harvested just before they reach maturity and hung up to air-dry. The foliage can be used fresh in arrangements and allowed to dry out naturally, or hung up to air-dry.

HELICHRYSUM *bracteatum*
monstrosum
STRAW FLOWER
Half-hardy Annual

Helichrysum is one of the best known species of everlasting flower. It is easy to grow and dry, available in a range of colours, and deservedly popular with beginners and experienced flower arrangers alike. It holds its colour well after drying.

Helichrysum can grow to 3 ft (1 m) high but dwarf 12–15 in (30–37.5 cm) varieties are available and especially useful where growing space is limited. Select the double-flowered varieties.

Many colours are available: golden yellow, lemon yellow, white, orange, purple, red, light pink, dark pink and salmon. The light pink is deservedly popular in wedding arrangements. The dark purple is marvellous at giving visual depth to complement lighter colours. Red is, of course, ideal for Christmas decorations.

Before selecting the colours to grow, consider the colouring of other flowers

that you intend to dry. For instance, choose dark pink *Helichrysum* to contrast with light pink larkspur, salmon with green grasses, lemon with pale blue statice, etc.

GROWING HINTS

Sow under glass in early spring or in the open in late spring. An ideal spacing for the larger plants is 6–10 in (15–25 cm) apart. *Helichrysum* like full sun and a well-drained soil. The problem with establishing them in a flower garden is

Helichrysum bracteatum

that they need to be picked in bud so their colour outdoors cannot be fully enjoyed. If intensive cropping is envisaged sow them in a separate plot, perhaps in the vegetable garden.

HARVESTING AND DRYING

Beginners invariably harvest *Helichrysum* too late, waiting until the flowers are fully open, so that by the time they are dry they have over-matured. It is best to pick them in the morning when the buds have just started to open, i.e. the outer layer of petals has opened but the centre is still a 'bud' shape. If cut when the central part of the flower is visible it will develop quickly and may open too far while drying and not look so attractive. Once the main flower has been picked, side shoots will develop, providing an extended harvesting period.

If the flowers have strong stems they can be bunched and hung up to dry and then used in arrangements as they are, provided they will not be placed in a damp atmosphere. If *Helichrysum* is allowed to reabsorb moisture after drying, the stems become too weak to support the heads, which will droop. For this reason, and because some stems are naturally weak, many people wire *Helichrysum* when they are fresh and then let them dry. Wiring later can be tedious as the centre of the flower becomes very hard. At the end of the season any tiny flowering heads remaining can be used in pot pourri.

If some of the flowers open out fully during drying and others remain in tight bud, try placing the large open flowers lower down and the small buds higher in an arrangement, thus giving a very natural progression of form.

HELICHRYSUM *subulifolium*
HELICHRYSUM

This variety of *Helichrysum* does not have the double flower of *H. bracteatum* but is a bright yellow against light green foliage.

Growing to about 12–15 in (30–37.5 cm) tall, it flowers throughout the summer and can be used as a fresh or dried flower, harvested just as it reaches full flowering.

HELLEBORUS *corsicus*
CORSICAN HELLEBORE
Evergreen Perennial

Helleborus corsicus is a very valuable edging and ground cover plant for shaded borders. It has dark green, leathery, prickly edged leaves. In winter and spring it carries large clusters of cup-shaped, pale green long-lasting flowers, growing to 1–2 ft (30–60 cm) in height.

GROWING HINTS
The hellebore is best purchased as a plant and located in good well-drained soil in a shady sheltered position. Once established it will grow quickly and seed freely, so give it plenty of room.

HARVESTING AND DRYING
Cut in late spring and hang up to air-dry very slowly. The petals will shrivel somewhat while drying but the flower head will, nevertheless, remain a fresh green and be useful as a background filler in arrangements.

HORDEUM *vulgare*
BARLEY
Annual Grass

Barley is an annual agricultural cereal grass, produced for the malting industry and as a livestock feed. It has long distinctive whiskers, or awns, on the ear which, as it matures, arches over. Most barley crops are 'two-rowed' — having two rows of seed in each ear or flower — but the 'six-rowed' varieties have fuller, more attractive ears for flower arranging.

GROWING HINTS
Barley would only be worth growing if in a small separate plot in the garden. When buying seed, check whether it is an autumn or spring sown type. (Six-row varieties generally require autumn sowing.)

Mildews, rust and other diseases can cause problems by discolouring the leaves.

HARVESTING AND DRYING

Barley is one of the first grasses to come into ear in late spring. Wait until the whiskery head has fully emerged beyond the leaves, but cut before the anthers emerge and the pollen is released if you want to capture the fresh green colour.

Alternatively, leave the head to mature and arch over and harvest in summer when it is naturally golden. This latter stage is most appropriate for harvest festival decorations.

In the green stage, fast drying is necessary to hold the colour, and it is wise to ensure the bunches are not too large. Hang upside down to dry and make sure the awns are not bent. Once dry, the awns become brittle. Bunches harvested when mature and golden will naturally be more dry and can be finished off slowly, standing upright.

HUMULUS *lupulus*

HOP

Deciduous Perennial Climber

The hop is a vigorous climber growing up to 20 ft (6 m) in summer and dying back below the ground in winter. It is dioecious — bearing male and female flowers on separate plants. It is only the females that bear the attractive cone-like flowers. These contain essential oils and bittering acids used in brewing beer. Hops are traditionally associated with herbal remedies for insomnia — hence hop pillows! The clusters of flowers are very pretty and natural-looking in arrangements and can be used in bridal head-dresses and posies in the early autumn. The commerically produced full length 'bines', about 10 ft (3 m) long, are popular as wedding or party decorations wound around marquee poles, columns or over church doors. In the house they can be hung along old beams, unsightly pipework, over fireplaces (providing they are not close enough to become a fire hazard), above old dressers or along the top of kitchen units. For festive occasions they can be made into colourful swags by tying in bunches of other dried flowers.

GROWING HINTS

Hops prefer a deep rich soil to give them vigour, and must be given a structure to climb up. Commercially they are grown up coir strings, with two or three young shoots encouraged to twine up each string and the others removed. In the garden they will scramble up through trees or over a trellis. The golden hop, *H. lupulus* 'Aureas', can be very effective as contrast foliage. Cut back to ground level in late autumn and feed well in spring. Hops are susceptible to aphids

Humulus lupulus

and certain mildew diseases which may affect the foliage colour in some seasons.

HARVESTING AND DRYING

The flowers start to show in mid-summer, but it is necessary to wait until they are fully developed in late summer or early autumn before cutting otherwise they will shrivel during drying.

The hop flowers are produced on side branches, or laterals, up to 18 in (45 cm) long. These sprigs can be picked and dried, or used fresh in arrangements and allowed to dry out naturally. The characteristic scent of hops can be quite strong for a few weeks after picking. Similarly, the full-length bines can be hung in position when fresh or semi-dried. Once fully dry the flowers become very brittle and should not be disturbed.

HYDRANGEA *macrophylla*
MOP-HEAD HYDRANGEA
Deciduous Shrub

Hydrangeas are frequently and easily grown in gardens, yet are not commercially grown in sufficient quantity to make them readily available for purchase as dried flowers. As a garden plant or dried flower they are invaluable. The colours of the fresh flowers vary from whites and pinks to blues, the difference being caused primarily by the nature of the soil — pink on alkaline or lime soils and blue on acid or clay ones. Flowers in shade tend to be green. The intensity of the colours deepens as the flowers reach maturity and when dried can make a wonderful display on their own or be an excellent background filler.

GROWING HINTS

For drying, be sure to select the sterile mop-head 'Hortensia' varieties (such as Altona, Hamburg and General Vicomtesse de Vibraye) rather than the lace-cap varieties.

Hydrangeas prefer a moist soil in a position of partial shade, but once established can grow well in full sun or in containers. During hot, dry weather keep the plants well watered. Flowers that have wilted will be of poor quality. Make sure they are in a position where their autumn colour can be appreciated.

Hydrangeas can be grown easily from cuttings. They will benefit from regular feeding and grow up to 5–6 ft (1.5–2 m) in height. A special additive composed of iron and aluminium can be bought to feed hydrangeas which, on lime soils, can suffer from mineral deficiencies. This additive alters the flower colouring from pinks towards blues.

HARVESTING AND DRYING

Timing the picking of hydrangeas correctly needs experience plus an awareness of changes in the weather. Hydrangeas picked too early will shrivel. Leave them too late and they will be ruined by the first frost or by wet weather.

As the hydrangea heads mature in the autumn, they gradually change and intensify in colour. To the touch they change from feeling soft, damp and cold to firm, dry and papery. Pick them at this stage and hang or stand them up to dry slowly. Fast drying will shrivel the petals. It will take several weeks to dry out the stems completely but, once dry, the flowers will hold their form and colour well as long as they are not in sunlight.

If early frosts threaten, pick the heads even if they are not quite ready, then stand them in a little water in a vase and leave them to dry out slowly.

Hydrangeas are sensitive to frost and a hard winter can damage the following year's flower buds. It is wise, therefore, to select flowers for drying with care and leave at least half of them on the bush for winter protection. Further pruning to remove dead heads can be done in the spring, as necessary, when the danger of late frosts is over.

HYDRANGEA paniculata

'Grandiflora'

HYDRANGEA
Deciduous Shrub

This particular variety is worth a special mention. In colour it is creamy white with a pink tinge. The form of the flower head is not globular but lilac-shaped and the individual florets are smaller than the hortensias. Both its colour and size make it particularly useful as a garden or dried flower. The full head can be used as a feature in large arrangements or small clusters of florets removed for use in daintier displays.

Harvesting and drying principles are the same as for other hydrangeas.

IRIS foetidissima

STINKING IRIS
Evergreen Perennial

Do not be put off by the name. The smell of stinking iris — likened to burnt rubber — is only associated with the roots or the bruised foliage. It has mauve or yellowy-green flowers but its main feature is its bright orange seeds held in the open seed pod through autumn and early winter. A bunch of these pods on their own can make an attractive display, or they can be incorporated in autumnal arrangements.

GROWING HINTS
The iris grows readily from seed and should be established in clumps in shade. It will tolerate quite heavy shade. It grows to about 1–2 ft (30–60 cm).

HARVESTING AND DRYING
Cut just after the pods have split open to reveal the shiny berries, and hang upside down to air-dry. The berries will eventually shrivel but their colours will remain strong.

KERRIA japonica 'Flore Pleno'

JEW'S MALLOW
Deciduous Shrub

Kerria japonica is an easily grown shrub which sends up suckers of arching green stems, soon forming a large clump about 6 ft (2 m) high. The variety 'Flore Pleno' has double yellow flowers in spring. It should be cut when the maximum number of flowers are in full bloom, bunched and hung up to air-dry.

LAGURUS ovatus

HARE'S TAIL GRASS
Annual Grass

Hare's tail is a popular ornamental grass, both for the garden and in dried arrangements. It has a small, soft fluffy head, growing to 1–2 ft (30–60 cm) in height. It can be dyed successfully, though it is a shame to spoil the soft grey/green colour of the best early-cut specimens. Use dyes only on the paler sun-bleached heads.

GROWING HINTS
Hare's tail can be sown in pots in early spring or in the garden a little later. Establish in clumps in a rockery or the front of a border. Being a native of Mediterranean regions it survives well in dry locations, but benefits from watering during early establishment.

HARVESTING AND DRYING
Cut when the hare's tail is full and fluffy, around flowering time. Alternatively, leave it on the plant to fade naturally in the sun if it is to be used for dyeing. The stems are very fine so bunches will be small. Hang up to air-dry, keeping the bunches separate from one another. Similarly, if boxing them for storage, separate layers of bunches with tissue paper to prevent the heads tangling.

LAURUS nobilis

BAY

Evergreen Shrub

Bay trees, often grown as small container shrubs for the patio, provide leaves that can be dried for use either in cooking or small arrangements, such as wreaths or flat wall posies. They are best picked during the autumn or winter and will dry easily in any warm location (a kitchen is ideal).

Bay trees also make large background or screening shrubs. They are tolerant of hard pruning but are liable to frost damage in severe winters.

LAVANDULA spica

LAVENDER

Evergreen Shrub

A selection of lavenders is available in pink and white as well as the traditional blue. All can be used for drying in bunches or the flower heads can be harvested separately for aromatic use. When growing for arrangements choose varieties with large full buds densely packed on long flower spikes, and as dark a blue as possible (e.g. *L. spica* 'Hidcote Giant' and 'Munstead'). A big bunch of lavender can be attractive on its own as a decoration but can also be a useful contrast with larkspur, red roses, lemon-yellow *Helichrysum*, etc. Lavender is best used as clusters of stems wired together, rather than as single spikes.

GROWING HINTS

Lavender can be grown from seed, though germination may be erratic, and can easily be propagated from cuttings. It likes a well-drained soil in full sun and is best used in the front of the border or as a low hedging plant. It is ideal for patios. Do not overfeed. Hard pruning in the spring will create longer-lived, more compact plants.

HARVESTING AND DRYING

To dry bunches, the lavender needs to be cut early, just before the buds open to show the tiny flowers. Hang and dry it gently or it will become brittle. For use in pot pourri, leave it later and then the flowers can easily be stripped from the stems.

LIATRIS spicata

L. callilepis

GAYFEATHER

Deciduous Perennial

Liatris has bright purple flower spikes growing from 1–2½ ft (30–75 cm), above fine narrow leaves. Unlike most flower spikes the buds start to open from the top downwards. The strong colour and form make *Liatris* a useful plant in combination with grey foliage and white and pink flowers (especially pink larkspur).

GROWING HINTS

Liatris likes full sun and does well in poor, light soils. It can be grown from seed or propagated by division.

HARVESTING AND DRYING

Cut when about half the head is in flower but before the top flowers mature too far. If left longer they may go to seed while drying. *Liatris* has a robust stem and can be dried upright or hanging. It holds its colour well and is dry when the base of the stem snaps when bent.

LIMONIUM latifolium

SEA LAVENDER

Hardy Perennial

Limonium latifolium is a finer and more delicate form of *L. tartaricum dumosa*, with smaller flowers and less rigid stems. Growing conditions are the same but it

reaches about 2 ft (60 cm) and has tiny
flowers with violet blue centres. *L.
latifolium* should be picked when the
flowers are fully open. It dries easily and
quickly and is less prickly to use than *L.
tartaricum dumosa*. Even when dry it can
retain a strange musty smell.

Limonium sinuatum

LIMONIUM *sinuatum*

(syn. *Statice sinuata*)

STATICE
Half-hardy Annual

Statice and *Helichrysum* are the two best
known everlasting flowers. Growing to

1–2 ft (30–60 cm) high, statice is available in many colours — white, pink, blue, purple, yellow and apricot (the latter can be very variable in shade, ranging from peachy yellow to raspberry pink). All the colours are bright (except the apricot) and last a long time. The white and blues tend to be the sturdiest to use and the yellow has the most brittle flower heads.

GROWING HINTS

Sow direct into open ground in late spring or raise under glass earlier. Statice is native to Mediterranean regions so tolerates full sun and dry locations, and it prefers an alkaline soil. The leading shoot can be picked out before flowering to increase the growth of side shoots. Statice can be grown either in a border where its bright colour can be appreciated or in a special plot if many plants are needed. It is well suited to locations of limited space.

HARVESTING AND DRYING

The flowers are papery and naturally dry easily, keeping their colour well. Nevertheless, it is a good idea to dry them in the dark as this retains the green stem colour and keeps them looking fresh.

Pick when all the flowers have opened and dry slowly or they will become brittle. Bunch loosely so the stems can be easily separated for use after drying, without damaging the heads. Rain tends to discolour the bright pink variety.

LIMONIUM *suworowii*

POKER STATICE

Half-Hardy Annual

Poker statice is very distinctive. It has densely packed, tiny pink flowers on a thin wavy spire that may be branched. The stems grow to about 18 in (45 cm), of which 10 in (25 cm) can be covered in flowers. They are unusual and fun to use.

GROWING HINTS

Sow in the spring in full sun. Poker statice tolerates most soil types and dry conditions, though stems will be much shorter if too dry.

HARVESTING AND DRYING

It flowers in mid to late summer and should be cut when the spike is in full colour — allowing the stem to gain as much length as possible but before the lowest flowers begin to lose their colour. Bunch and air-dry hanging upside down. The stems are fine but strong and easy to use in arrangements.

LIMONIUM *tartaricum dumosa*

SEA LAVENDER

Hardy Perennial

Sea lavender is universally popular as a background filler in dried flower arrangements. It forms a dense low mass, 1 ft (30 cm) high, of branched flowering stems above a rosette of dark green leaves. The tiny flowers are like white stars with pink centres when fully open.

GROWING HINTS

Sown in spring, it will flower in its second summer. It is a robust plant surviving in most conditions and soil types. In the garden it should be grown at the front of the border, but could also be established in gravel around patios.

HARVESTING AND DRYING

Wait until all the flowers are fully open but pick before the pink centres start to go brown and while the stems are still green. Sea lavender is the easiest of all plants to dry and in warm weather will need little help to dry out completely. Nevertheless, make sure the stems are dry before storing and do not crush the bunches at any stage or the stems will become distorted and tangled.

Sea lavender takes dye easily and the softer colours of pink, lavender blue, pale yellow and peach are very useful in arrangements.

LINUM *usitatissium*
LINSEED
Annual

Linseed is an agricultural crop grown for its oil-rich seeds. It is closely related to flax, and grown in some regions for its tough, fibrous stems used in the production of linen. It grows to 2–3 ft (60–100 cm) tall and, in fields, is identifiable in mid-summer by its flushes of pale blue flowers which appear in the morning and last only a day, having lost their delicate petals by evening.

GROWING HINTS
When buying seed do not confuse it with other garden *Linum* species, which are unsuitable for drying. Sow in spring in open ground. In the garden allow it to establish in dense patches for the best effect.

HARVESTING AND DRYING
Linseed has quite a long harvesting period, from mid-summer, when the immature seed pods are green among a few late flowers, until late summer when all the flowers have developed into spherical pods. As the plant matures, the colour of the seed pods changes from green to yellow and eventually, by early autumn, both seed pods and stems will be brown.

The young green stage is best chosen for a fresh look. The yellow stage tones well with harvest-coloured arrangements, and the mature brown pods can be sprayed gold or silver for Christmas decorations. Take care when harvesting because a sharp knife or pair of secateurs will be needed to cut the fibrous stems.

Because the seed contains oils, drying it properly is not straightforward. An initial bout of drying in warm air is needed to hold the green colour of the stems and leaves, but then a long period of slow drying is necessary to ensure that the pods can be kept and stored successfully. If not fully dry, mould will develop. Crush individual pods and rub them between a finger and thumb to test for dryness. To assist the drying process do not pack too many stems in each bunch and, when storing, keep the bunches separate to prevent tangling. The seeds are very attractive food to mice so dry, store and display linseed in a safe place.

LONAS *inodora*
AFRICAN DAISY
Annual

Lonas grows from 12–18 in (30–45 cm) high and has clusters of bright yellow button flowers on the top of a strong stem. In colouring it is like the much larger *Achillea filipendulina*, but its scale makes it useful in small arrangements. It looks good in contrast to orange *Helichrysum* or blue statice.

GROWING HINTS
The plants enjoy a sunny position in well-drained soil. Sow in open ground in late spring.

HARVESTING AND DRYING
Lonas flowers in mid-summer and should be cut as soon as it is fully open. Hang the bunches upside down to air-dry.

LUNARIA sp.
HONESTY
Biennial/Perennial

Honesty has always been popular for winter dried flower arrangements because of its silvery white oval seed pods. In the garden it looks best in an informal situation, and either white or violet-purple flowering varieties can be used (or the type with variegated leaves). Biennial

(*L. biennis*) and perennial (*L. rediviva*) varieties are available.

GROWING HINTS

Honesty grows easily from seed and will spread freely. It prefers light shade. Sow in late spring to flower the following spring/early summer.

HARVESTING AND DRYING

The seed pods develop on stems about 2–3 ft (60–100 cm) high. These can be picked early and dried to retain their greenness. If left, their green colour gradually fades to silvery-white and the flat discs of the pods become dry and papery. Timing of picking at this stage is not critical but the seed heads are fragile and can be damaged by wind and torn if left too long. The two outer discs of the pod can be removed by rubbing the pod gently between a finger and thumb to reveal the shiny, almost translucent, inner disc. Save the flat brown seeds.

Honesty needs very little drying — only enough to make sure the lower part of the stems are brittle. Handle with care once fully dry, and store out of

Matricaria 'Snow Puffs'

reach of mice, for whom the seed heads make wonderful bedding material.

MATRICARIA *eximia*
FEVERFEW
Half-hardy Annual

Flowers in the *Matricaria* family are similar to small spray chrysanthemums in form. Dwarf varieties make good edging plants. The white, double-flowered *Matricaria* dries successfully to a form similar to *Achillea ptarmica* 'The Pearl'. The herb feverfew has small daisy-like flowers, white with a yellow centre, and can also be dried.

GROWING HINTS

Sow under glass in early spring and plant out after the late frosts. Once established, feverfew seeds freely. Plants will grow up to 3 ft (1 m) in height.

HARVESTING AND DRYING

Cut when in full flower and dry hanging upside down.

MATTHIOLA sp.
STOCK
Half-hardy Annual

The double-flowered stocks can be dried with moderate success to give an effect similar to larkspur. Pick when in full flower and dry quickly in a warm place. They hold their scent very well and produce some delightful musky colours. Unfortunately, however, they tend to absorb moisture and the stems go limp easily, so may require wiring.

MISCANTHUS sinensis
MISCANTHUS GRASS
Perennial Grass

The tall, ornamental miscanthus grasses, growing to 6 ft (2 m) tall, are useful plants for the middle or back of the border. The pinky-brown flowering plumes appear in late summer and last into the winter.

For drying, pick when the flowering plumes have fully emerged but before they are damaged by autumn weather.

MOLUCCELLA laevis
BELLS OF IRELAND
Annual

Always popular with fresh flower arrangers, Bells of Ireland can be dried successfully, though need to be handled carefully as the bells break off easily. The bells are pale green calyces, containing little white lemon-scented flowers. In the garden the colour shows up well against a dark background.

GROWING HINTS
Sow under glass in early spring or in open ground in late spring. The stems grow to 3 ft (1 m) tall and may need support. Bells of Ireland like a moist soil.

HARVESTING AND DRYING
The flowers appear in late summer and, for drying, the stems should be cut when the bells have become firm to the touch. To retain the fresh green colour it is necessary to pick before the lower bells begin to fade. Fresh young bells at the top of the stem will probably not have 'set' by this stage; they will shrivel during drying and need to be trimmed off. Alternatively, the stems can be left longer to fade and bleach naturally in the sun, though discoloration will occur from rain. Always remove the leaves before drying. Tie only a few stems in each bunch and hang to dry slowly. Handle carefully when dry, but keep any fallen bells as they can be used for interesting effect in small arrangements or collages (secured by glue). Try spraying them with gold or silver to make Christmas decorations. Bells of Ireland can also be preserved by glycerining.

NARCISSUS sp.
DAFFODIL
Bulb

Certain varieties of double-flowering daffodils can be dried successfully, such as 'Golden Ducat', but the problem with them is that the stems are very fleshy, take a long time to dry out fully and then will quickly reabsorb moisture in a damp atmosphere. Drying in silica is more successful.

NICANDRA physaloides
SHOO FLY PLANT
Hardy Annual

The value of *Nicandra* to dried flower arrangers lies in its seed, which is reminiscent of Chinese lanterns (*Physalis*

Moluccella laevis

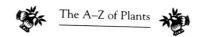

franchettii) but pale green in colour. The flowers, which appear in summer, are pale lilac-blue bells.

GROWING HINTS
Nicandra can be grown easily from seed sown in the open in spring. It has a bushy growth up to 3 ft (1 m), so needs plenty of space.

HARVESTING AND DRYING
As with most other seed pods it is necessary to let the pods mature before picking, otherwise they will shrivel when dried. They can be picked while still green or allowed to fade on the plant, and dried slowly either upright or hanging. Remove the leaves before drying.

NIGELLA *damascena*

LOVE-IN-A-MIST
Hardy Annual

Love-in-a-mist is a delightful annual with its fine leaves and delicate flowers of pink, blue or white. It can be dried in full flower but the most useful part of it is the seed pod. Picked at the right stage, the pod is green with stripes of dark maroon, surrounded by a finely-cut tracery of leaves. (The blue flowered 'Miss Jekyll' variety has a good seed pod colour.) In arrangements the dark stripe is a marvellous complement to pink or red and the head fits well into either small or large displays. It is an essential part of any dried flower garden and is

Nigella damascena

ideal where there is limited space.

More unusual, interestingly shaped seed pod varieties, such as the yellow-flowered *N. orientalis* 'Transformer', are being developed specifically for drying but seeds may be more difficult to purchase.

GROWING HINTS
Sow in autumn or spring. Germination can be very slow in dry conditions but, once established, *Nigella* will self-seed freely. It likes most soils and a position in full sun, and will flower in early to mid-summer. It grows 1½–2 ft (45–60 cm) high.

HARVESTING AND DRYING

The seed pods are at their best three to four weeks after flowering. Wait until the pods have developed to their full size but have not started to fade in colour. If picked too early, the pods will shrivel during drying.

If cut at the early flowering stage rapid drying is necessary to prevent petal drop, but if cut later the seed pods will air-dry easily (and the seeds can be collected for the next year's sowing). If left longer the pods will dry naturally on the plant but will fade considerably.

ORIGANUM dictamnus

syn. O. marjorana

SWEET or KNOTTED MARJORAM
Annual

A useful plant for the herb garden, sweet marjoram can be used in cooking and as a filler in dried flower arrangements. It grows to only 10 in (25 cm) tall and is grey-green in colour with minute white flowers forming in green bobbles up the stem (hence the 'knotted' appearance).

GROWING HINTS

Sow in late spring in open ground in full sun.

HARVESTING AND DRYING

Cut bunches of stems as low to the ground as possible and hang up to air-dry in the kitchen where the aroma will be appreciated.

ORIGANUM vulgare

POT MARJORAM or OREGANO
Perennial

Pot marjoram grows wild in sunny dry locations, especially on chalk. The dark pink flowers are very attractive to bees and butterflies and dry easily for use in

Origanum vulgare

small arrangements. The leaves can be used in cooking.

GROWING HINTS

The plants grow from 12–18 in (30–45 cm) tall and can be established in the herb garden or flower border. (The shorter golden-leaved variety 'Aureum' makes a bright edging plant.) Sow in spring in an open position.

HARVESTING AND DRYING

Harvest when just about to break bud or in full flower and hang up to dry. A kitchen always seems the most appropriate place for drying herbs!

PAEONIA sp.

PEONY

Deciduous Perennial

Peonies are glorious plants for the herbaceous border, flowering in late spring or early summer. They are widely used as cut flowers and though not easy to dry are magnificent when successful. When dried they can be mistaken for a full-blown English rose and, in arrangements, add a touch of great distinction.

GROWING HINTS

Peonies can be grown from seed, but since they take a few years to bloom well, they are best purchased initially as small plants and grown in rich, deep soil in sun or light shade. The flower buds can be damaged by late frosts so a sheltered position is advisable. Once established, do not transplant as the roots dislike disturbance. The double *P. officinalis* varieties, available in white, pink and crimson red, are the earliest to flower, in late spring. 'Rubra plena' dries to a magnificent rich dark red.

The double pink *P. lactiflora* 'Sarah Bernhardt' is the most popular commercially grown variety, but the double white variety 'Duchesse de Nemours'

dries equally well. Both flower in late spring or early summer.

P. tenuifolia has simple red flowers with bright yellow stamens and dries very well.

HARVESTING AND DRYING

The harvesting stage is critical. Peonies open very quickly in warm sunny weather and within a day can have developed too far to dry successfully.

Double peonies As the bud swells, the outer petals open but the centre mass can still be firm and hard. These central petals then unfurl and it is important to cut the flower as soon as the centre is soft and the stamens are visible, but before it has opened enough to reveal the young seed pod at the centre. If the outer petals start to reflex the flower has matured too far and attempts to dry it will only result in a hanging stem and a heap of petals on the floor!

Single peonies Allow the flower to open fully to display the yellow anthers but cut before the petals reflex. Remove all but the top one or two leaves (to speed the drying process), tie not more than five in a bunch (or the heads may be crushed) and hang up to dry quickly in warm air. Slow drying may result in the flower maturing too far and the petals dropping during later use. Do not despair, however, if early attempts at drying fail — the petals are lovely in pot pourri!

Peonies can be prone to insect damage after drying. Eggs laid in the young flower (particularly of later flowering varieties) can survive even high-temperature drying and hatch out during storage, allowing larvae to eat away the base of the petals and making the flower eventually disintegrate. If infestation is suspected, putting the dried flowers in the deep freeze for 48 hours and then into a warm atmosphere will usually solve the problem! If the flower head becomes squashed or mis-shapen during drying or storage, holding it over the steam from a kettle for a short while will enable the petals to soften and expand.

PANICUM *miliaceum*

COMMON MILLET or BROOM-CORN MILLET

Annual Grass

Millet is an annual grass of agricultural importance grown particularly in the Far East and used in wholefoods and cage-bird seed. *Panicum miliaceum* is yellowy-green and grows 3–4 ft (1–1.2 m) high. It has a pendulous, weeping form which is not only attractive in the garden but is superb in dried arrangements. Most dried flowers are necessarily stiff in form, but this millet adds softness and movement to arrangements. *P. violaceum* is an ornamental purple-tinged form.

Papaver somniferum

GROWING HINTS
Millet requires warm, moist soil to germinate and become established so it is best sown in late spring in full sun. Cultivate it in groups in the garden.

HARVESTING AND DRYING
Wait until the loose panicle head has fully emerged from the stem and then harvest. If left too long the seeds will start to develop, colour will begin to fade and there will be a problem of the seeds being shed after drying. Tie in small bunches and hang to air-dry fairly rapidly to hold the colour. Once dry, keep millet out of the reach of mice!

PAPAVER sp.

POPPY

Annual

Papaver somniferum is available in either 'mini' or 'maxi' sizes, but it is the latter

which is most impressive and useful in arrangements. Because it is harvested at the seed pod stage its flowers can be enjoyed in the garden through the summer. The flowers are large, papery and whitish-mauve, with a dark base to the petals. They grow to about 2½ ft (75 cm) tall and the seed pods are large, round and a biscuity-grey colour. They have a strong form for use in arrangements and look particularly good in contrast to deep purple *Helichrysum* or red *Amaranthus*.

P. somniferum 'Hen and Chickens' has a curious seed pod composed of a central round pod surrounded at the base by a dense ring of smaller heads — hence the name. (In some countries it is illegal to grow *P. somniferum*.)

P. rhoeas, the common red field poppy, has small elongated seed pods which can be used in clusters in delicate arrangements. The tall and colourful double-flowered garden varieties have larger pods which are more useful.

P. nudicaule should be avoided for drying because it is poisonous.

GROWING HINTS
The tiny seeds should be sown in spring in a fine moist soil. Establish in groups in full sun against a dark background to enjoy the full benefit of the flowers.

HARVESTING AND DRYING
Drying poppies in the flowering stage is generally unsuccessful as the petals drop easily. Enjoy the display of flowers and wait for the seed pods to swell to their full size. The pods are green initially but mellow and develop a matt-grey patina with maturity. This is the best time to harvest. If picked too early the pods will shrivel when dried; if left too late they will discolour. The pod will seem almost dry by the time it is harvested but further drying is advisable to ensure that the thicker part of the stems, and the centre of the seed pod, are fully dry, otherwise mould may develop later.

Hang or stand up to air-dry — somewhere out of reach of mice and where it does not matter if the seeds drop out.

PHALARIS canariensis
CANARY GRASS
Hardy Annual Grass

The short, fat, arrow-shaped heads of canary grass make it particularly useful in arrangements. Commercially it is often available in dyed colours but the natural green is very attractive. It can be tall, growing to 3–4 ft (1–1.2 m).

GROWING HINTS
Sow in spring to flower in the summer. Establishment in the autumn can result in larger flower heads but a hard winter or late frosts can kill off young plants or cause discoloration. Canary grass will self-seed if some heads are left uncut in the autumn.

HARVESTING AND DRYING
Cut soon after the heads have emerged while still tight in form. The seed head will expand as the seeds inside develop but colour loss will occur with maturity. Unwanted leaves can be stripped to reduce the bulk for drying. Air-dry upside down quickly if you want to retain the best colour.

PHLEUM pratense
TIMOTHY GRASS or MEADOW CAT'S TAIL
Perennial Grass

Timothy is a common perennial grass of agricultural importance in traditional hay meadows. The flower head is a thin dense cylindrical spike, and grows 3–5 ft (1–1.5 m) high. It is frequently to be found growing on road verges. Its pencil-like form can add interesting texture or give direction to arrangements.

GROWING HINTS

Sow in summer or autumn to flower the following year in early summer. The grass develops into clumps and is shallow rooting, so prefers moist soils.

HARVESTING AND DRYING

Cut as soon as the flowering spike has emerged beyond the leaves, while it is still green. Strip off any unwanted leaves. Air-dry upside down and store carefully to ensure the flower spike is not bent. Use in natural 'country' arrangements.

PHLOMIS *fructicosa*

P. 'Edward Bowles'

JERUSALEM SAGE
Evergreen Shrub

Phlomis is a shrub growing up to 4 ft (1.2 m) tall. It has soft grey-green leaves and whorls of yellow flowers. The flowering stems can be dried but it is the brown seed heads at the end of the season which have a particularly strong

form for use in arrangements. *P.* 'Edward Bowles' is the smaller of the two varieties suggested here, growing up to 3 ft (1 m), but has larger leaves.

GROWING HINTS

Plant in a sunny position in well-drained soil. The colouring blends well with white borders.

HARVESTING AND DRYING

Cut when in full flower and hang up to dry, or leave until the seed heads have developed fully and turned brown. Picked at the later stage, the stems need very little additional drying and can be stood upright.

PHYSALIS *franchettii*

CHINESE LANTERN
Deciduous Perennial

Chinese lanterns are popular and easy to grow, but very expensive to buy because they are not widely commercially grown.

In autumn the bright orange seed heads are unmistakable. When dried, they make a lovely display just on their own or mixed with other plants of strong form such as grey eucalyptus leaves and *Allium christophii* seed heads.

GROWING HINTS
Physalis seed is readily available and should be sown under glass in early spring or in a warm place in late spring or early summer. It may take several weeks to germinate. The plants should then be grown on in a well-drained and sunny position where they have adequate space to spread. The long underground roots will rapidly help the plant form a large clump, growing to 2 ft (60 cm) in height. Propagate by division in spring.

HARVESTING AND DRYING
The insignificant white flowers appear in early summer and develop into the lantern-shaped seed pods which are green at first, later changing to orange. The stems should be cut in the autumn when as many as possible of the lanterns are orange but before the plant is damaged by frost or rain. The leaves should be removed. The bunches will air-dry easily and should be laid in open boxes. Alternatively, stand upright in a well-ventilated or warm place.

POLYGONUM *bistorta*

P. amplexicaule

KNOTWEED
Deciduous Perennial

Polygonum bistorta is a very useful ground cover plant, having leaves similar to docks (*Rumex*) but with tall, pink-flowering spikes in late spring and early summer. It grows to a height of 1½–2 ft (45–60 cm). *P. amplexicaule* is taller, growing up to 4 ft (1.2 m) high, with larger crimson spikes.

GROWING HINTS
Polygonum likes light shade with a moist soil. It is naturally invasive and will have to be kept under control where space is limited.

HARVESTING AND DRYING
Cut when in full flower and hang up to air-dry.

ROSA sp.

ROSE
Perennial Shrub/Climber

The dried roses generally available for purchase are invariably of the type grown commercially for cut flower use, with small heads. Many other types of garden roses can be successfully dried to marvellous effect and have a completely different look to the commercial roses. Often a few well-placed roses in an arrangement can be the perfect finishing touch, providing essential focal points for a colour scheme and adding a feeling of quality to a display.

So many different varieties of rose are available that it would be pointless to make specific recommendations. Besides, it is worth experimenting with all types! For small dainty arrangements, the tiny spray roses and small-headed bud roses can be used. For larger arrangements select the double flower types — preferably those that have the full-blown 'Old English' look. Garnette roses are especially recommended for drying.

Flower colours often change or intensify during drying. Red roses usually hold their colour well though some can finish very dark. Rich yellows look good initially but can go dull quickly. Peach, dark pinks and purples dry well, but some of the paler pinks can be unpredictable and fade quickly. White roses can dry surprisingly well, though very high temperatures will cause discoloration at the base of the petals. However, some people like the "antique" look of faded roses!

GROWING HINTS

It is impossible to summarize in one paragraph all the intricacies of rose growing! Suffice it to say that they generally require a deep, rich soil, management to eradicate pests and diseases, and regular pruning. Further detailed cultural advice should be sought on individual varieties. The shrub and botanical species types are generally more trouble-free.

HARVESTING AND DRYING

In the garden, pick the roses as the flowers begin to open and fill out in shape, but before they reach their full flowering glory. Strip off the thorns from the base of the stem if necessary, but do not remove the leaves as these can be used as a dark green filler.

Keep the bunches small to prevent damage to the flowers and hang up to dry as quickly as possible in warm air. Once fully dry the stems can become very brittle, so roses should always be the last items added to a display so they are not accidentally damaged. The heads can, of course, be wired if necessary. Rose petals or small rose heads are lovely in pot pourri.

ROSMARINUS officinalis
ROSEMARY
Evergreen Perennial

Rosemary is a lovely scented herb to grow in the garden and use in cooking. It needs a warm sunny location and a well-drained soil. Some varieties can grow up to 6 ft (2 m) tall but the smaller ones are ideal for patios, border edges or informal hedges. The flowers — blue, white or light pink — appear in late spring.

Sprays of the foliage, with or without flowers, can be cut to hang in the kitchen for culinary purposes or to use in arrangements. The leaves are brittle when dry so it is advisable to make decorative use of the rosemary as soon as possible and let it dry fully in position without disturbance.

SALVIA horminum
syn. S. sclarea
CLARY
Hardy Annual

Clary is a small bushy border plant growing to 18 in (45 cm) high and noticeable for its brightly coloured bracts ranging from greenish-white and pink to purple. It provides a lasting splash of colour in the garden throughout the summer and can then be cut and dried. Because of this, it is a useful annual for small gardens and around patios.

GROWING HINTS

Sow outdoors from late spring onwards in clumps. Alternatively, raise under glass and transplant out in late spring to avoid frost damage. Clary needs full sun and, for drying, is best grown in a poor soil.

HARVESTING AND DRYING

Avoid the temptation to harvest too soon and wait until the coloured bracts have stiffened a little and become firm. Tie in small bunches and hang up to air-dry slowly. Fast drying can make the leaves shrivel.

SALVIA officinalis
COMMON SAGE
Evergreen Shrub

The common sage has an undramatic purple/blue flower spike and soft grey-green leaves which are strongly aromatic and used in cooking. Small bunches of the leaves can be cut and dried in autumn for a background filler in arrangements.

GROWING HINTS

Sage needs full sun and a well-drained soil. Growth needs to be pruned back to prevent the bushes sprawling and becoming untidy.

HARVESTING AND DRYING

Cut the leaves in autumn when they are less likely to shrivel during use. Tied in small bunches, they will air-dry easily, hung in a kitchen.

SANTOLINA chamaecyparissus
LAVENDER COTTON
Evergreen Shrub

Santolina has dense, aromatic, silver-green foliage and yellow button-like flowers in summer. It is a useful plant for the front of the border or small hedges, but needs pruning in spring. Like the curry plant, *Helichrysum angustifolium*, both flowers and foliage can be dried.

GROWING HINTS

Plant in a warm sunny position on well-drained soil and prune hard in spring to maintain fresh young growth. *Santolina* can be propagated from cuttings.

HARVESTING AND DRYING

The flowers appear on thin stems in mid-summer. Cut when in full flower and hang up to air-dry. The foliage will dry easily hung up in small bunches or may be used fresh in arrangements and allowed to dry in place naturally.

SCABIOSA stellata
S. 'Paper Moon'
S. 'Satellite'
SCABIOUS
Hardy Annual

Scabious 'Paper Moon' is a hardy annual with unusual papery seed heads on long strong stems. The soft lavender blue flowers are a delight in the herbaceous border, especially in informal planting schemes, and can be enjoyed to the full since it is only the later seed heads which are cropped.

GROWING HINTS

Sow outdoors in spring in full sun or plant out seedlings 6–9 in (15–22.5 cm) apart. Scabious will grow well in ordinary well-drained soils but occurs naturally on lime. It can develop 20–30 flower stems on a single plant, growing up to 3 ft (1 m) high, so should be located in the middle of a border with adequate space to flourish.

HARVESTING AND DRYING

The seed heads develop rapidly after flowering. If harvested while still a pale green they will look better than if left to mature on the plant. Rain can quickly cause discoloration. Keep bunches small to prevent damage to the individual heads, which are very fragile and should be handled as little as possible. Very little drying is needed.

SEDUM spectabile
ICE PLANT
Deciduous Perennial

Many members of the *Sedum* family are low-growing plants suited to rock gardens, but the *Sedum spectabile* varieties, such as 'Autumn Joy', are taller growing, reach-

Sedum spectabile 'Autumn Joy'

ing 1½–2 ft (45–60 cm). They make a reliable flowering contribution to the herbaceous border from late summer to mid-autumn and are popular with bees and butterflies. The leaves are fleshy and pale green and the tiny pink flowers are held in flat-topped clusters on long stems. The flowers dry to a dark dusky pink.

GROWING HINTS
Plant in a sunny well drained position near the front of the border. Once established, *Sedum* can be easily propagated by division or cuttings.

HARVESTING AND DRYING
Pick in the autumn, waiting until the flower heads have developed enough to become firm. The stems are fleshy and take a very long time to dry. Strip the leaves, tie small numbers of stems together and hang up to air-dry in a warm place. (Leaves and side shoots can still develop while the flowers are drying.) Do not store until the stems are completely dry otherwise they will go mouldy. Alternatively, the flowers can be used straightaway and left to dry naturally, provided the arrangement is to be kept in a warm, dry room.

SENECIO *greyi*

S. *laxifolius*

SENECIO
Evergreen Shrub

Senecio is a handsome evergreen, grey-leaved shrub with daisy-like yellow flowers in summer. It grows up to 5 ft (1.5 m) tall. Sprays of the foliage make a useful filler in flower arrangements, especially in contrast to deep pinks.

GROWING HINTS
Plant senecio in full sun in well drained soil. It is reasonably hardy but may suffer damage in severe winters. Prune hard in spring to prevent it becoming too woody and straggly. Senecio can be easily propagated from cuttings.

HARVESTING AND DRYING
Cut sprays of foliage in the autumn or winter and hang up to dry in small bunches. The leaves will curl a little but this does not detract from their value as a soft grey filler. Alternatively, use them fresh and allow to dry naturally in position in an arrangement.

SETARIA *italica*

ITALIAN MILLET
Annual Grass

Setaria is an annual grass and there are many varieties, including S. *lutescens* which is a smaller, yellowy version. The size of the heads differs according to the variety, but the very large fat heads are commonly used as food for cage-birds. The charm of S. *italica* lies in its fresh colour, retained when dried. It looks particularly attractive with pink larkspur.

GROWING HINTS
Sow in full sun in late spring to ensure warm soil temperatures.

HARVESTING AND DRYING
Cut soon after the flower heads have emerged and developed in size, but before the colour starts to fade. Colour retention is important so hang up to dry quickly in warm air, in the dark.

SOLIDAGO *canadensis*

GOLDEN ROD
Deciduous Perennial

Golden rod is a deciduous perennial bearing plumes of bright yellow flowers over bright green foliage on stems that range from 2–6 ft (60 cm–3 m) high, depending on the variety. It can spread to form large clumps. Harvested at the correct stage its fresh colouring is most useful in arrangements complementing yellow roses, *Lonas* and *Achillea filipendulina*, or contrasting with pure white gypsophila and deep blue larkspur or lavender.

The taller varieties are particularly useful in large arrangements, perhaps with *Echinops* and bright green millet.

GROWING HINTS
Golden rod can be established in any soil but tolerates poor dry soil well, in sun or light shade. It can be raised from seed sown in spring or propagated by division.

HARVESTING AND DRYING
Cut the stems in summer as (or just before) the first flowers begin to open. Do not wait until they are in full flowering colour as the heads will burst into seed very quickly during drying and the fresh yellow will be lost. It is better to pick too early than too late.

Hang up to dry quickly in warm air so as to retain the greenness of the leaves and halt the development of the flowers.

TAGETES *erecta*
AFRICAN MARIGOLD
Half-hardy Annual

The large, orange and yellow double-flowered African marigolds, which make colourful bedding plants, can be easily dried. They should be picked in the early stages of full flower and hung up to air-dry. The flowers will shrink but retain their dense colour well. The base of the flower head at the top of each stem tends to be weak and wiring may be necessary. The flowers are rarely suitable as focal points, but provide strong colour.

TANACETUM *vulgare*
TANSY
Deciduous Perennial

Tansy, a herb which self-seeds freely in the garden, can be used as a dried flower.

Sprays of small neat yellow flowers can be left on their stems for tall arrangements or used separately for more delicate work, especially with fresh greens and white.

TRITICALE
BEARDED WHEAT
Annual Grass

Triticale is a hybrid between wheat (*Triticum*) and rye (*Secale*). The ears have whiskers, or awns, giving them a softer appearance than wheat, but the awns are shorter and less brittle than those of barley. It can be used in natural arrangements or to make sheaves, but the effect is generally soft and feathery whereas wheat is strong and sculptural.

Cultivation and harvesting instructions are as for wheat. It has very good natural disease resistance and is grown as an agricultural cereal where drought tolerance is necessary.

TRITICUM *aestivum*
COMMON WHEAT
Annual Grass

Wheat, grown as an agricultural crop for bread and biscuit making, is an extremely useful element in dried flower arrangements because of its strong form. It can also be used on its own to make ornamental wheatsheaves which give a 'country' feel to any decorative scheme.

GROWING HINTS

Autumn- and spring-sown varieties are available in agricultural use and should be cultivated accordingly. If wheat is to be grown in the garden it is best established in its own plot. The young plants develop grass-like tillers initially, but in late spring growth is rapid as the stem extends to 2–3 ft (60–100 cm).

HARVESTING AND DRYING

As soon as the ear of wheat appears in late spring or early summer, it starts to flower. If cut too early the bunches will have too leafy an appearance and the ears will be small, but as soon as the plant has flowered, the green colour begins to fade from the ear and leaves, to become the familiar golden harvest colour of full summer. Wheat should be cut either at flowering time (when the ear is level with the leading 'flag' leaf) for the best green colour or left until the golden stage.

At the green stage the plant contains substantial reserves of sap. It should be tied in thin bunches and hung up to dry as quickly as possible.

The golden stage requires little additional drying and the rigid stems can be stood upright. Keep dried wheat out of the reach of mice!

TULIPA sp.

TULIP
Bulb

As with daffodils, tulips are not an obvious subject for drying and are difficult to dry successfully. However, there are some colours and varieties with which it is worth experimenting. The late double peony-flowered tulips have sufficient density of petals to be effective and the darker colours will be most successful. The parrot tulips have fringed and twisted petals, some are variegated and they can all look extraordinary.

Of the single tulips the paler colours are unlikely to dry or last successfully, so choose the dark pinks, reds or, especially, the purples.

HARVESTING AND DRYING

Tulips should be cut in the early stages of flowering and hung up to dry in very warm air. The stems are fleshy and take a very long time to dry. Even after thorough drying they will readily re-absorb moisture from a damp atmosphere and go limp. Tulips should always be wired after drying to support the stems or arranged so that the heads are supported by surrounding flowers.

TYPHA latifolia

BULRUSH or REEDMACE
Deciduous Perennial

Bulrushes grow naturally beside streams and ponds and in waterlogged areas. They spread rapidly and should not be introduced into a new pond without careful thought or strict management to contain their growth. However, bulrushes that are already available in the garden can be dried to make impressive displays on their own, or with other tall seed heads such as teasel.

HARVESTING AND DRYING

The problem with bulrushes is to stop the cylindrical brown heads bursting into seed. They should therefore be cut as soon as they have turned brown, in mid-summer, and air-dried as quickly as possible. (The terminal spike above the head should be trimmed off before drying to improve the appearance.) If the leaves are to be retained the stems should be hung up to dry. If not, they can stand upright.

Bulrushes grow up to 7 ft (2.2 m) in height, so plenty of space is needed for drying and displaying.

XERANTHEMUM *annuum*

EVERLASTING FLOWER
Hardy Annual

Xeranthemum has daisy-like flowers with petals that are naturally stiff and straw-like. It is available in white, dusky pink, rose pink, lilac and purple. (The white and strong pinks are very useful.) It can look delightful sown in drifts in informal garden schemes and flowers successively in summer. The flowers can be dried easily and used individually in dainty arrangements, massed in bunches in larger displays, or mixed with grasses for a very informal 'country' effect. No wiring is needed.

GROWING HINTS
Select double-flowering varieties and sow in spring in full sun. *Xeranthemum* will grow adequately on poor soils. The plants form small clumps of greeny-grey foliage. Flowering height is 1½–2 ft (45–60 cm).

HARVESTING AND DRYING
Xeranthemum flowers in late summer to early autumn. Initially, pick single stems on which the flowers have opened fully, tie in small bunches and hang up to dry. This early crop provides flowers that can be used individually.

As more buds break into flower, there will come a stage when it is worthwhile cutting handfuls of stems at a time. These bunches will include open and half-open flowers, as well as buds. This variation within a bunch gives it a very natural look but more drying is needed with the bunches hanging in warm air. (The young closed buds will always tend to absorb moisture and become limp so display these only in a dry atmosphere.)

Timing of harvesting is not very critical but as the flowers age they discolour and can be damaged by rain. Discard all such flowers as they will spoil the overall effect.

ZEA *mays*

MAIZE, SWEETCORN, CORN
Annual Grass

Maize is an annual grass of agricultural value in the production of grain, and certain types are sown as a fresh vegetable. It grows 5–7 ft (1.5–2.2 m) in height. The fruiting cob is yellow in the common edible varieties, but multi-coloured and miniature variants are also available for ornamental use.

GROWING HINTS
Sow in late spring in full sun. The large seed will easily emerge from 2–3 in (5–7.5 cm) below the soil surface, therefore sow deep enough to utilize the moisture available.

HARVESTING AND DRYING
Maize plants bear the male flowering parts, or anthers, at the top of the stem. This light, biscuit-coloured plume can be an unusual item when dried — useful as a filler or background in medium-sized or large arrangements. Remove the top 2–2½ ft (60–75 cm) of the maize plant and hang up to air-dry in warm air in the dark, so as to retain the greenness of the leaves.

Later in the autumn, the familiar cob with its tightly-packed seeds can be picked for drying. Wait until the fleshy seeds have hardened (much beyond the edible stage!) and the cob has started to dry out naturally on the plant. (This reduces the tendency of the seeds to shrink and shrivel.) Allow plenty of time for the cobs to dry out fully and, once dry, store away from mice in a dry ventilated place. The leaves around the cob can be peeled back as part of the ornamental effect.

DRIED FLOWER ARRANGING

One of the joys of growing and drying your own flowers is that there is only the cost of your own time to take into account. When buying bunches of dried flowers for a basket this size, you can easily spend large amounts of money and still not achieve the full look you wanted.

In this arrangement there are eight bunches of a peachy rose called 'Gerdo', several bunches of light and dark blue delphiniums, four bunches of white larkspur, *Achillea ptarmica*, various types of statice and some *Eryngium*, or sea holly. With a basket this size, it is very important to introduce some strong splashes of colour, which can be created by bunching several flower heads of the same type together.

Fill the basket with dry florists' foam and then a covering of *Limonium tartaricum dumosa*. This hides the rather dull-looking foam and forms a base for the arrangement. Then add the longer items, such as the delphiniums and larkspur, to create the outline shape. Once the overall outline is achieved you can fill in with clumps of the various components until the basket looks really full and impressive.

It is far better to create something very special that will be much admired than to be mean with your material and produce many small, insignificant arrangements with the absolute minimum of ingredients. As is mentioned in earlier chapters, many of the larger items you can easily grow in the garden are the most expensive to buy commercially, so make the most of your collection of flowers and create a really eye-catching display.

One of the most pleasurable points about arranging with dried flowers is that it opens up a much wider choice of containers than one would have with arrangements of fresh flowers. As there is no need for water you can make up arrangements in porous containers that leak if filled with water, or precious boxes and baskets that are too valuable to be used with water even if lined!

A lavish basket of roses and delphiniums can bring summer into the house all year round.

Florists' foam

The most popular way to arrange dried flowers is perhaps by using the grey-brown florists' foam intended specifically for dry arrangements. There is a brighter green counterpart for fresh arrangements. This foam is easily sliced and shaped to the size of container you wish to use, and holds the stems firmly in position. It can be reused. Another popular alternative is insert the stems in a ball of clay that hardens after a while. Although perfectly satisfactory, it is far harder to use than florists' foam, and cannot be reused. Squashed chicken wire is another alternative which is particularly useful for large containers and arrangements. Some very ambitious large-scale arrangements, say, in an enormous fireplace, could use up a great many blocks of foam, and so filling the container with squashed chicken wire is considerably cheaper.

Arranging without mechanics

Another possibility is demonstrated opposite — using no mechanics at all. In this terracotta container the flowers have been kept in the original bunches in which they were dried or bought. The taller bunches are placed in position first at the back of the container, and the others are grouped in tiers to show off each variety to its best advantage. Some manoeuvring can take place, with strategic bunches being made larger or smaller in order to obtain the desired effect. When the majority of the container is full, single items such as the artichokes are arranged as the bottom tier to cover any stems that might be visible.

The overall effect of an arrangement of this kind is a bold display of colours, shapes and textures, giving the eye plenty to look at. The informal nature of the arrangement particularly suits terracotta containers of this type or alternatively you could use basket-ware or other containers with a rural feel.

The actual flowers and plants used in this display include wheat, *Phlomis*, bulrushes, *Allium* heads, poppies, *Amaranthus*, *Alchemilla* and linseed, artichokes and marjoram to name but a few. The seed heads in the centre of the display are *Iris foetidissima*.

As you can see from the photograph, this type of arrangement is far from economical with flowers and materials. If you had to buy all the bunches used in this terracotta container then it would be an extremely expensive arrangement. If, however, you have had a successful year growing these plants in your garden and then drying them, it can be a pleasure to have such a splendid excuse to show off a reasonable number of bunches from your collection.

Casual arrangements can make a fantastic impact if they are strong enough and are carefully accessorized.

FIREPLACE ARRANGEMENT

Once you have mastered smaller and simpler arrangements, decorating an area like a fireplace can be a real challenge. There are many ways to tackle it. The photograph opposite shows a formal way of filling a fireplace when it is not in regular use. There are other equally effective ideas, such as an informal arrangement in a large hamper or basket, a terracotta container similar to the one shown on the previous page, or natural features such as wheat sheaves and hop bines to give a harvest atmosphere to the room.

A great many flowers went into this arrangement, but again, if the material has been home-dried you are saving a considerable amount of money. The base is a large basket which has been packed with blocks of dry florists' foam taped together to prevent them slipping. The basic shape is made with air-dried eucalyptus and *Carthamus*, then pale blue delphiniums are introduced around the edge and through the design. Apricot *Limonium sinuatum*, 'Gerdo' roses and salmon *Helichrysum* are then added to give an attractive contrast and warmth to the arrangement.

A splendid array of flowers like this can be put together without incurring a great deal of expense, if you grow the flowers yourself.

IDEAS FOR CONTAINERS

There are many attractive containers on the market today which enable you to have a refreshing change from the standard table-top arrangement. Apart from interesting shapes such as cornucopias, hampers, ducks and boxes, there are many varieties of wall-hanging containers that offer plenty of scope for unusual arrangements of your collection of dried materials.

The particular container used in the arrangement opposite has a narrow pocket into which you can place dry florists' foam ready for an arrangement. Here, a collection of cream and gold flowers and grasses has been used. They include millet, roses, *Helichrysum* and *Achillea ptarmica* 'The Pearl'. It is a very monochromatic colour scheme that provides a restful change from some of the stronger colour combinations and effects that are equally exciting. This tranquil arrangement might look attractive in a bedroom decorated in creams and pinks or peaches.

There are other shapes and styles that can be wall-hung. One that immediately springs to mind is a dried flower wreath or garland. These are somewhat trickier to make but look extremely pretty in any room in the house.

Once you have a good selection of materials to work with, your eye will automatically spot new ideas for containers, whether at jumble sales, in auction rooms or shops and markets selling modern pieces. Since they do not have to be waterproof you can let your imagination run riot.

The same rule applies to accessories. If you are making an arrangement for a bathroom, then why not include some shells, stones or pebbles? These can be attached with glue or wire around the edge of the container. Carrying a theme through an arrangement can be great fun, whether it's for a kitchen, using wooden spoons as an ingredient, or something arty in a studio including some sable brushes!

Keeping an open mind and generally being observant will bring many new ideas into view. There are plenty of lovely natural accessories to introduce into arrangements, such as mosses, cones and berries, shells, driftwood, stones and sea-washed lumps of glass. If you have no fixed view of what will and won't be suitable then all sorts of items will spring to mind. Just be prepared to have a large cupboard full of objects that are bound to be useful one day!

This gentle arrangement of colours would tone well with many colour schemes.

VICTORIAN-STYLE ARRANGEMENT

Many suitable containers may well be lurking in your cupboards. This vegetable tureen is not part of a set and is only ever used for flower arrangements. The base was filled with dry florists' foam and taped securely. The lid was then carefully stored away so that it was neither lost nor damaged while the base was in use elsewhere.

This particular arrangement has a very light, frothy effect with the mass of *Gypsophila* that has been used. The base flowers are red peonies, silver rose *Helichrysum* and pink roses, with some *Limonium sinuatum*. The arrangement could well have stood on its own without the *Gypsophila* but the delicate touch it adds is very pleasing. This particular style of display would look pretty anywhere, but perhaps a bedroom would be the best place. This type of design is also useful for wedding arrangements and displays.

If a flower arrangement looks a little strong in colour for the room in which you want to display it, then adding white can be a very quick way to lighten the colours. Either *Gypsophila* or *Achillea ptarmica* 'The Pearl' both have a similar effect. Since *Gypsophila* is so easily available and simple to dry, it can be a very easy choice for dainty displays.

This antique tureen makes a perfect container for a soft and dreamy arrangement.

ARRANGEMENTS FOR WEDDINGS

Dried flowers are becoming increasingly popular for weddings, and with good reason. Arranging the flowers, if fresh, always has to be a last-minute job, and the pressure of decorating houses or a church when one has a million other things to do as well can be tremendous. Even if a professional is doing the flowers for you, there is always the worry that they won't appear when they should! With dried flowers you can create arrangements, bouquets, pew ends — anything, in fact — many weeks beforehand and store them carefully as you finish them.

If you plan to take on the flowers for a family or friend's wedding then obviously you will have to decide what needs to be grown, and which plants will be ready to harvest and dry before you want to start work on them. The basic colour scheme is obviously the main choice to be made, plus the style of arrangements. You can plan formal arrangements like the one featured in the photograph opposite or something far more countrified, using swags of oats and other cereals, trailing hop bines, baskets and other rustic containers.

Brides and bridesmaids look very pretty with circlets of dried flowers on their heads, and if a bouquet is made from dried flowers then it can be kept forever. The most popular colour scheme for weddings of late must surely have been peaches and cream. Although this is a wonderfully subtle colouring that suits every bride, it can look far more exciting and eye-catching if stronger colours are used. In the display shown here, very strong purples are mixed with cream, gold and pink for a really stunning effect.

Many people seem to think that dried flowers are all pale colours or have an orange and beige bias to them, but this particular display proves how mistaken they can be. This selection of colours is just as bright and vibrant as a fresh arrangement would be. The flowers used were cream peonies (very rarely available commercially and so beautiful), *Limonium sinuatum*, roses (both 'Bridal Pink' and a pale pink called 'Porcelina'), millet, *Helichrysum* and pink larkspur.

There is never any need to waste anything with dried flower work, and should you have any spare petals there are plenty of ideas for using them on pp. 114–19, including a recipe for the wedding confetti.

Planning dried flowers for a wedding can be a much easier alternative to fresh flowers, as they can be arranged many weeks beforehand.

TABLE CENTRE ARRANGEMENTS

Table centres are always a very decorative way to finish a festive table. The design shown here could blend with several colour schemes and can be brought out as and when it is needed.

The base is an oval piece of cork on to which a small green plastic florists' attachment, known as a 'frog', is glued. The florists' foam is then impaled on this 'frog'. Two special candle holders are then inserted into the foam to take the candles, which are made slightly different heights by sawing off a length from the bottom of the second candle before it is used.

A wide variety of material has been used. The plant material includes eucalyptus, iris seed heads, tansy, carnations, *Celosia*, *Solidago*, *Aquilegia* seed heads, poppies, *Matricaria*, *Craspedia* and hydrangeas. The shape will partly be governed by the size of your table and the amount of space available.

If you are short of space, then instead of making a large table centre some very small posy arrangements could be placed on each side plate, or small arrangements glued to some wooden napkin rings. Narrow garlands also look stunning ranged down the centre of the table.

A long-lasting table centre made from a selection of dried garden flowers.

USING LEFT-OVER DRIED FLOWERS

If a great deal of time and effort has been expended in getting your dried flower stocks together, then you will want to waste as few of them as possible. No matter how careful you are there will always be occasions when you break a head off its stem, some petals fall out or other accidents befall you. A perfect way to use every little scrap of material is to make up bright and colourful bowls of pot pourri with any damaged or discarded pieces.

There is no limit to what you may include in your personal pot pourri mix: as long as the finished result smells beautiful and looks attractive, the ingredients are to some extent irrelevant. A number of recipes are listed here to start you off with ideas and give you a base to experiment with, but the real fun starts when you adapt recipes to suit yourself.

Home-made pot pourri is fun to make and smells wonderful.

Basic pot pourri

This basic recipe is very versatile and the ingredients can be interchanged depending on which left-overs you have available at the time. Use a measuring jug to obtain the correct volume of ingredients. Orris root powder is available from chemists or health food shops.

> 1 pint (600 ml) dried rose petals
> ½ pint (300 ml) dried peony petals
> ¼ pint (150 ml) dried mint leaves
> ¼ pint (150 ml) dried geranium leaves
> 6 tbsp (90 ml) roughly crushed cinnamon sticks
> 5 tbsp (75 ml) dried orange and lemon peel, roughly crushed
> 1–1½ oz (5–7.5 ml) orris root powder
> 6 drops rose essential oil

Mix together all the ingredients, except the essential oil, in a large dry washing up bowl or mixing bowl until they are evenly dispersed. Add the oil drop by drop. Then fill a plastic bag with the mixture and tie the top into a tight knot. Leave it in a cool dark place for about five to six weeks, giving it a vigorous shake about twice a week.

Once the mixture is ready to use it can be displayed with some whole flower heads placed around the edge of the container or scattered on the surface of the mixture for additional decoration.

Blue Moon pot pourri

> 1 pint (600 ml) dried cornflower flowers
> ¼ pint (150 ml) dried pale blue larkspur flowers
> ¼ pint (150 ml) dried dark blue larkspur flowers
> ¼ pint (150 ml) dried blue/lavender Limonium sinuatum flowers
> ¼ pint (150 ml) dried eucalyptus leaves
> 6 tbsp (90 ml) roughly crushed star anise, nutmeg and
>   ginger
> 5 tbsp (75 ml) dried lime and grapefruit peel, roughly chopped
> 1–1½ oz (5–7.5 ml) orris root powder
> 6–8 drops lemon verbena or rose geranium oil

Again, mix together all the ingredients except the oil, and then follow the instructions given in the previous recipe.

Autumn pot pourri

1 pint (600 ml) small dried orange/red Helichrysum *heads*
½ pint (300 ml) small cones such as larch
¼ pint (150 ml) small red/gold autumn leaves, pressed
¼ pint (150 ml) acorns
12 cinnamon sticks, cut in three
5 tbsp (75 ml) chunky-cut dried orange peel
4 drops orange essential oil
4 drops cinnamon essential oil
slices of dried apple for decoration

Again mix together all the ingredients and proceed as in the previous recipes. If you wish, you can use a little extra oil and drop it deep into the opened scales of the cones as they will retain the smell beautifully. This mixture can look lovely placed in a large basket surrounded by cones and miniature bundles of wheat and oats with dried slices of apple in between.

Cottage garden pot pourri

This recipe is perfect for using really miscellaneous left-overs. It looks best if you can get some colour co-ordination or blending, but alternatively why not go for broke and have a really brightly coloured mix!

2 pints (1.2 l) dried mixed flowers and petals
10 tbsp (150 ml) mixed chunky spices and herbs
1–1½ oz (5–7.5 ml) orris root powder
8 drops any oil of your choice!

Follow the instructions given in the previous recipes, choosing whichever ingredients you wish to use.

When using the essential oils it is sometimes more successful to use one type only at a time but you can experiment by mixing a few together, particularly if you have only a few drops left in several bottles. If you find your recipe has been a great success then do remember to write down what your proportion of ingredients and oils were as you may not remember should you wish to repeat it!

As well as using oils in pot pourri you can also sprinkle them carefully on to dried flower arrangements, fairly deep down in the display. A bowl of cones sprinkled with essential oils always looks attractive and only takes a few seconds to prepare. (The scent is stronger if you add the oil to the cones and then keep them in a bag for six weeks as mentioned in the basic pot pourri recipe). If you are arranging a hop bine as part of a room decoration then some hop flowers are bound to fall off. They make a pretty pot pourri on their own with essential oils, so they need not be wasted.

Natural confetti

Another possibility for petals, especially peony and rose petals, is to make scented or unscented natural wedding confetti. So many churches, hotels and other places are against the throwing of highly-coloured and dyed paper confetti because of the mess it creates that it seems a good alternative to return to real rose petals that will decompose naturally and look far more attractive.

For the wedding confetti, you can use any petals that blend with the overall colour scheme at which you are aiming. If you want some petals to be flat and some curled then a few fresh petals that have dropped naturally from some roses could be pressed while the fresh roses are being dried. Peony petals, in particular, are very large and have wonderfully strong colours. If you want to scent the confetti then place the collection of petals into a polythene bag and add several drops of whichever essential oil you prefer. The confetti should then be left for at least a week or two before it is used.

Many other ingredients, apart from flower heads and petals, can be included in a pot pourri mix. In the photograph on pp. 114–15 the pot pourri includes cinnamon sticks, dried apple slices, hops and pine cones. Shells look attractive mixed with flowers and there are many citrus mixes that include orange or lemon peel.

Another attractive feature is a large bowl or basket full of rose heads — perhaps using both the commercial and old-fashioned varieties, with a few miniature ones added for good measure. Dishes to hold the pot pourris or other ideas are easily made by glueing dried flowers and ribbons around a tiny basket or dish before filling it with the pot pourri.

Spring fragrance

> *1 pint (600 ml) dried narcissus heads (ideally dried in silica gel)*
> *1 pint (600 ml) dried apple blossom*
> *1 pint (600 ml) myrtle leaves*
> *1 pint (600 ml) eucalyptus leaves*
> *2 oz (50 g) orris powder*
> *10–14 drops lily of the valley oil*

Mix all ingredients as in previous recipes.

Many seed pods and cones hold essential oils very well and can be scented and displayed alone. A large basket of pine cones, scented with a suitable essential oil, looks very attractive on a large hearth.

Strawberries and cream

  1 pint (600 ml) strawberry leaves dried
  1 pint (600 ml) pale pink globe amaranth flowers
  1 pint (600 ml) dark pink globe amaranth flowers
  1 pint (600 ml) cream globe amaranth flowers
  2 oz (50 g) orris powder
  12 drops strawberry fragrance oil

Mix all ingredients as in previous recipes.

Traditional Christmas

  1 pint (600 ml) larch cones
  1 pint (600 ml) roughly snapped cinnamon sticks
  ½ pint (300 ml) star anise
  ½ pint (300 ml) allspice berries
  1 pint (600 ml) dried rose hips
  1 pint (600 ml) conifer or spruce leaves
  3 tbsp (45 ml) dried orange peel
  2–3 oz (50 g–75 g) orris root
  5 drops pine essential oil
  5 drops cinnamon essential oil
  5 drops orange essential oil

Mix all ingredients as before. This pot pourri looks particularly attractive in a large shallow basket edged with pine cones, red and green tartan bows, spruce sprigs and miniature Christmas tree baubles. Make a Christmas feature of this pot pourri on a hall table to welcome guests with a traditional fragrance.

APPENDIX I
Flowers grouped according to their colour

All the major species in the A–Z section are listed here under the predominant flower colour. When available in two or three colours they are listed accordingly, but if more, the plant is shown as being available in a selection of colours.

Available in a selection of colours

Acroclinium roseum	Sunray	*Gomphrena globosa*	Globe amaranth
Aquilegia hybrida	Columbine	*Helichrysum bracteatum*	Straw flower
Aster sp.	Aster	*monstrosum*	
Astilbe arendsii	False goat's beard	*Hydrangea macrophylla*	Mop-head hydrangea
Centaurea cyanus	Cornflower	*Limonium sinuatum*	Statice
Chrysanthemum sp.	Chrysanthemum	*Matthiola* sp.	Stocks
Clematis sp.	Clematis	*Nigella damascena*	Love-in-a-mist
Dahlia sp.	Dahlia	*Papaver* sp.	Poppy
Delphinium consolida	Larkspur	*Rosa* sp.	Rose
Delphinium elatum	Delphinium	*Salvia horminum*	Clary
Dianthus barbatus	Sweet William	*Tulipa* sp.	Tulip
Dianthus caryophyllus	Carnation		

Blue/Mauve

Acanthus mollis	Bear's breeches	*Lavandula spica*	Lavender
Agastache mexicana	Agastache	*Limonium latifolium*	Sea lavender
Campanula glomerata	Clustered bellflower	*Linum usitatissium*	Linseed
Cynara cardunculus	Cardoon	*Nicandra physaloides*	Shoo fly plant
Cynara scolymus	Globe artichoke	*Nigella damascena*	Love-in-a-mist
Echinops ritro	Globe thistle	*Papaver somniferum*	Annual poppy
Eryngium sp.	Sea holly	*Scabiosa stellata*	Scabious

Brown

Alnus glutinosa	Common alder (cones)	*Fagus sylvatica*	Beech (leaves and seed cases)
Centaurea macrocephala	Knapweed (seed cups)	*Miscanthus sinensis*	Miscanthus grass
Corylus avellana contorta	Corkscrew hazel (stems)	*Phlomis fruticosa*	Jerusalem sage (stems)
		Typha latifolia	Bulrush

Crimson/Red

Amaranthus sp.	Love-lies-bleeding	*Celosia argentia cristata*	Cockscomb
Atriplex hortensis 'Rubra'	Orach	*Paeonia* sp.	Peony
		Polygonum amplexicaule	Knotweed

Green

Alchemilla mollis	Lady's mantle	*Festuca* sp.	Fescue grass
Amaranthus paniculatus	Love-lies-bleeding	*Helleborus corsicus*	Corsican hellebore
Ambrosinia mexicana	Ambrosinia	*Hordeum vulgare*	Barley
Aquilegia hybrida	Columbine (seed head)	*Humulus lupulus*	Hop
		Lagurus ovatus	Hare's tail grass
Astrantia major	Masterwort	*Moluccella laevis*	Bells of Ireland
Avena sativa	Oat	*Origanum dictamnus*	Sweet or knotted marjoram
Briza sp.	Quaking grass		
Bromus sp.	Rye brome grass	*Panicum miliaceum*	Common millet
Carthamus tinctorius	Safflower (bud)	*Phalaris canariensis*	Canary grass
Cucurbita pepo	Gourd (fruit)	*Phleum pratense*	Timothy grass
Dactylis glomerata	Cocksfoot grass	*Setaria italica*	Italian millet
Dipsacus fullonum	Common teasel	*Triticale*	Bearded wheat
Euphorbia polychroma	Cushion spurge	*Triticum aestivum*	Common wheat

Orange

Carthamus tinctorius	Safflower
Iris foetidissima	Stinking iris (berries)
Physalis franchettii	Chinese lantern (seed pod)
Tagetes erecta	African marigold

Pink/Purple

Achillea millefolium 'Cerise Queen'	Yarrow	*Limonium suworowii*	Poker statice
		Lunaria sp.	Honesty (flowers)
Allium sp.	Onions, leeks, chives	*Origanum vulgare*	Pot marjoram
Armeria caespitosa	Thift	*Paeonia* sp.	Peony
Bergenia sp.	Bergenia	*Polygonum bistorta*	Knotweed
Dianthus x. *allwoodii*	Pink	*Sedum spectabile*	Ice plant
Calluna vulgaris	Heather	*Xeranthemum annuum*	Everlasting flower
Erica sp.	Heath		
Liatris spicata	Gayfeather		

White (Cream)

Achillea ptarmica	Sneezewort
Agastache urticifolia 'Alba'	Agastache
Ammobium alatum	Winged everlasting flower
Anaphalis margaritacea	Pearl everlasting
Calluna vulgaris	Heather
Carlina acaulis caulescens	Carline thistle
Carthamus tinctorius	Safflower
Cortaderia selloana	Pampas grass
Erica sp.	Heath
Gypsophila paniculata	Baby's breath
Hydrangea paniculata	Hydrangea
Limonium tartaricum dumosa	Sea lavender
Lunaria sp.	Honesty (seed pods)
Matricaria sp.	Feverfew
Paeonia sp.	Peony
Xeranthemum annuum	Everlasting flower

Yellow

Acacia decurrens dealbata	Mimosa
Achillea filipendulina	Yarrow
Anethum graveolens	Dill
Centaurea macrocephala	Knapweed
Clematis orientalis	Clematis
Clematis tangutica	Clematis
Craspedia globosa	Drumstick
Euphorbia polychroma	Cushion spurge
Helichrysum angustifolium	Curry plant
Helichrysum subulifolium	Helichrysum
Kerria japonica	Jew's mallow
Lonas inodora	African daisy
Narcissus sp.	Daffodil
Nigella orientalis 'Transformer'	Love-in-a-mist
Phlomis fruticosa	Jerusalem sage
Santolina chamaecyparissus	Lavender cotton
Senecio greyi	Senecio
Solidago canadensis	Golden rod
Tagetes erecta	African marigold
Tanacetum vulgare	Tansy
Zea mays	Maize (cobs)

APPENDIX II

Plants useful for their foliage

Anaphalis margaritacea	Pearl everlasting
Cotinus coggygria	Smoke tree
Eucalyptus sp.	Gum tree
Fagus sylvatica	Beech
Helichrysum angustifolium	Curry plant
Laurus nobilis	Bay
Rosmarinus officinalis	Rosemary
Salvia officinalis	Common sage
Santolina chamaecyparissus	Lavender cotton
Senecio greyi	Senecio

APPENDIX III

Grasses suitable for drying

The species listed below are all grasses whose appearance and value to the dried flower arranger are described individually in the A–Z section.

Avena sativa	Oat
Briza sp.	Quaking grass
Bromus sp.	Rye brome grass
Cortaderia selloana	Pampas grass
Dactylis glomerata	Cocksfoot grass
Festuca sp.	Fescue grass
Hordeum vulgare	Barley
Lagurus ovatus	Hare's tail grass
Miscanthus sinensis	Miscanthus grass
Panicum miliaceum	Common millet
Phalaris canariensis	Canary grass
Phleum pratense	Timothy grass
Setaria italica	Italian millet
Triticale	Bearded wheat
Triticum aestivum	Common wheat
Zea mays	Sweetcorn

APPENDIX IV

Flowers which can be dried at seed head stage

Several plants can be enjoyed throughout the summer in the garden, then later cut at seed head stage, for use in dried flower arrangements. Species which fall into this category are listed below, but for further details refer to the A–Z section.

Allium sp.	Onions, leeks, chives
Alnus glutinosa	Common alder
Anethum graveolens	Dill
Aquilegia hybrida	Columbine
Atriplex hortensis	Orach
Carlina acaulis caulescens	Carline thistle
Centaurea macrocephala	Knapweed
Clematis sp.	Clematis
Cynara scolymus	Globe artichoke
Cynara cardunculus	Cardoon
Dipsacus fullonum	Common teasel
Iris foetidissima	Stinking iris
Linum usitatissium	Linseed
Lunaria sp.	Honesty
Nicandra physaloides	Shoo fly plant
Nigella damascena	Love-in-a-mist
Papaver sp.	Poppy
Physalis franchettii	Chinese lantern
Scabiosa stellata	Scabious
Zea mays	Maize/sweetcorn

APPENDIX V

Plants that dry well with the silica gel method

A great many plants dry well with this method but as this book concentrates mainly on air-drying, this is a short list of particular favourites that benefit from drying in silica gel crystals.

Anemone coronari   Anemone   *Paeony* sp.   Peony
  and *A. elegans*   *Rosa* sp.   Rose
Fuschia hybrida   Fuschia
Helleborus orientalis
  and *H. niger*

Roses are especially successful, as are peonies. Old-fashioned roses look wonderful when dried with silica gel, but must be given false or wire stems to blend in with other large pieces of plant material that have been air-dried.

APPENDIX VI

Plants that can be preserved in glycerine

Again, this is not an exhaustive list but it gives a few favourites which can be very useful in arrangements, since air-drying does not work well for foliage.

Adiantum capillus-veneris	Maidenhair fern
Betula sp.	Birch
Buxus sempervirens	Common box
Calluna vulgaris	Heather
Choisya ternata	Mexican orange blossom
Eucalyptus sp.	Eucalyptus
Euphorbia robbiae	Spurge
Fagus sylvatica	Common beech
Garrya elliptica	Garrya
Hedera sp.	Ivy
Hosta sp.	Hosta
Moluccella laevis	Bells of Ireland
Polygonatum multiflorum	Solomon's seal
Quercus sp.	Oak
Rosa sp.	Rose

INDEX

Acacia decurrens dealbata, 46
Acanthus mollis, 46
Accessories, 106
Achillea, 9; *A. filipendulina*, 8, 15, 17, 46, 48; *A. millefolium*, 15, 47–48; *A. ptarmica*, 8, 9, 15, 48, 100, 106, 109
Acroclinium roseum, 48–49
African daisy, 82
African marigold, 97
Agastache, 17; *A. mexicana*, 18, 49; *A. urticifolia alba*, 18, 49
Air-drying, 34–37
Alchemilla, 9, 103; *A. mollis*, 49
Alder, common, 50
Allium, 9, 49–50, 103; *A. christophii*, 21, 50
Alnus glutinosa, 50
Amaranthus, 13, 103; *A. caudatus*, 50–52; *A. paniculatus*, 50–52
Ambrosinia, 15–18; *A. mexicana*, 52
Ammobium alatum, 52–53
Anaphalis margaritacea, 53
Anethum graveolens, 53
Annuals, 11–14
Antifreeze, 41
Aquilegia, 113; *A. hybrida*, 54
Armeria caespitosa, 54
Artichokes, 103
Aster, 54; *A. novae-belgii*, 54
Astilbe arendsii, 55
Astrantia major, 55
Atriplex hortensis, 55
Avena sativa, 55–56

Baby's breath, 73
Background material, 9
Barley, 75–76
Bay leaves, 15, 79
Bear's breeches, 46
Beech, 40, 71
Bells of Ireland, 14, 84
Bergenia, 56

Borax, 37
Briza, 56
Bromus, 56–57
Bulrushes, 98, 103

Calluna vulgaris, 57
Campanula glomerata, 57
Canary grass, 90
Cardoon, 64
Carlina acaulis caulescens, 57
Carline thistle, 57
Carnations, 68–69, 113
Carthamus, 9, 34, 105; *C. tinctorius*, 59
Celosia, 113; *C. argentea cristata*, 59
Centaurea cyanus, 59–60; *C. macrocephala*, 60
Chicken wire, 103
Chinese lanterns, 8, 21, 37, 91–92
Chives, 17, 49–50
Choisya, 40
Chrysanthemums, 60
Clary, 93
Clematis, 62
Clustered bellflower, 57
Cockscomb, 59
Cocksfoot grass, 66
Colour, 13, 28–32, 41, 120–2
Columbine, 54
Confetti, 118
Containers, 106
Corkscrew hazel, 62
Cornflowers, 14, 59–60
Corsican hellebore, 75
Cortaderia selloana, 62
Corylus avellana contorta, 62
Cotinus coggygria, 63
Craspedia, 13, 113; *C. globosa*, 63
Cucurbita pepo, 64
Curry plant, 18, 73
Cushion spurge, 71

Cynara cardunculus, 64; *C. scolymus*, 21, 64–66

Dactylis glomerata, 66
Daffodils, 84
Dahlias, 66
Daisies, 39
Delphinium, 15, 68, 100, 105; *D. consolida*, 14, 67–68; *D. elatum*, 68
Desiccants, 37–39
Dianthus × allwoodii, 68–69; *D. barbatus*, 68; *D. caryophyllus*, 68–69
Dill, 14, 18, 53
Dipsacus fullonum, 69
Drumsticks, 63
Drying techniques, 34–42
Dyes, 41

Echinops, 15; *E. ritro*, 69–70
Erica, 57
Eryngium, 70, 100
Eucalyptus, 8, 70–71, 105, 113
Euphorbia polychroma, 71
Everlasting flowers, 99

Fagus sylvatica, 71
False goat's beard, 55
Fescue grass, 27, 71–72
Festuca, 71–72
Feverfew, 83
Fireplaces, 105
Florist's foam, 103
Foliage, 9, 40–41, 123
Freesias, 37

Gayfeather, 79
Globe amaranth, 72
Globe artichokes, 21, 37, 64–66
Globe thistles, 15, 69–70
Glycerine, 35, 39–40, 125
Golden rod, 8, 96–97
Gomphrena, 13; *G. globosa*, 72

Gourds, 64
Graminaea, 72
Granny's bonnet, 54
Grasses, 27, 34, 72, 123
Gum trees, 70–71
Gypsophila, 17, 37, 109; G.
  paniculata, 73

Hare's tail grass, 78
Harvesting, 34
Heather, 57
Helichrysum, 8, 13, 14, 34, 105,
  106, 109, 111; H.
  angustifolium, 18, 73; H.
  bracteatum, 9; H.b.
  monstrosum, 73–75; H.
  italicum, 18; H. subulifolium,
  75
Helleborus corsicus, 40, 75; H.
  foetidus, 40
Herbs, 14, 15–18
Honesty, 8, 82–83
Hops, 76–77
Hordeum vulgare, 75–76
Humulus lupulus, 76–77
Hydrangea, 8, 9, 17, 37, 113; H.
  macrophylla, 77; H.
  paniculata, 78

Ice plant, 94–96
Insect damage, 42
Iris, 113; I. foetidissima, 78, 103
Italian millet, 96

Jerusalem sage, 91
Jew's mallow, 78

Kerria japonica, 78
Knapweed, 60
Knotweed, 92

Lady's mantle, 49
Lagurus ovatus, 78
Larkspur, 14, 67–68, 100, 111
Laurus nobilis, 79
Lavandula spica, 79
Lavender, 9, 15, 79
Lavender cotton, 94
Liatris spicata, 79
Lilies, 37
Limonium latifolium, 15, 79–80; L.
  sinuatum, 9, 14, 80–81, 105,
  109, 111; L. suworowii, 81; L.
  tartaricum dumosa, 15, 81–82,
  100
Linseed, 82, 103
Linum usitatissimum, 82

Lonas inodora, 82
Love-in-a-mist, 8, 14, 86–87
Love-lies-bleeding, 50–52
Lunaria, 82–83

Maize, 99
Marigolds, 97
Marjoram, 15, 87–88, 103
Masterwort, 55
Matricaria, 113; M. eximia, 83
Matthiola, 84
Michaelmas daisy, 54
Millet, 27, 89, 106, 111
Mimosa, 46
Mint, 15
Miscanthus sinensis, 84
Moluccella, 9; M. laevis, 84

Narcissus, 84
Nicandra physaloides, 84–85
Nigella, 14; N. damascena, 86–87

Oats, 27, 55–56
Onions, 49–50
Orach, 55
Oregano, 14, 87–88
Origanum dictamnus, 14, 87; O.
  vulgare, 87–88

Pampas grass, 27, 62
Panicum miliaceum, 89
Papaver, 89–90
Patios, 28
Pearl everlasting, 53
Peonies, 8, 15, 17, 23, 34, 88–89,
  109, 111
Perennials, 15–18
Phalaris canariensis, 90
Phleum pratense, 90–91
Phlomis, 103; P. fruticosa, 91
Physalis franchettii, 21, 91–92
Pinks, 68–69
Planting schemes, 28–32
Poker statice, 81
Polygonum bistorta, 92
Poppies, 8, 21, 89–90, 103,
  113
Pot pourri, 115–19

Quaking grass, 27, 56

Reedmace, 98
Rosemary, 18, 93
Roses, 8, 23, 38, 92–93, 100,
  105, 106, 109, 111
Rosmarinus officinalis, 93
Rye brome grass, 56–57

Safflower, 59
Sage, 18, 93–94
Salvia horminum, 93; S. officinalis,
  93–94
Sand, 37
Santolina chamaecyparissus, 94
Scabiosa stellata, 94
Scabious, 94
Sea holly, 70, 100
Sea lavender, 9, 15, 79–80, 81–82
Sedum spectabile, 94–96
Seed heads, 21, 124
Senecio greyi, 96
Setaria italica, 96
Shoo fly plant, 84–85
Silica gel, 35, 37–39, 125
Smoke tree, 63
Sneezewort, 48
Soil, 9
Solidago, 8, 113; S. canadensis,
  96–97
Statice, 14, 80–81, 100
Stinking iris, 78
Stocks, 84
Storage, 42
Straw flower, 73–75
Sunray, 48–49
Sweet william, 68

Table centre arrangements, 113
Tagetes erecta, 97
Tanacetum vulgare, 97
Tansy, 97, 113
Teasels, 69
Thrift, 54
Thyme, 15
Timothy grass, 90–91
Triticale, 97
Triticum aestivum, 97–98
Tulips, 98
Typha latifolia, 98

Varnish, 39
Victorian-style arrangement, 109

Weddings, 111
Wheat, 27, 97–98, 103
Wild gardens, 28
Winged everlasting flower, 52–53
Wiring flowers, 9, 38

Xeranthemum annuum, 99

Yarrow, 46–48

Zea mays, 99

ACKNOWLEDGEMENTS

Caroline Alexander would like to thank the following for their help in the production of this book:

William Alexander for his expertise and assistance in the preparation of the A–Z section, and for his kind permission to reproduce transparencies used to illustrate the A–Z section. Tom Wright for his horticultural advice.

Joanna Sheen would like to thank the following for their help in the production of this book:

Everyone at Joanna Sheen Ltd who helped when things got busy. Her family who as usual took all the strain. Jane Struthers for being there whenever she was needed and for helping to edit the manuscript. Ward Lock, especially Jane Donovan and Alison McWilliam, for being part of this project.

The publishers and authors would like to thank the following for their help in the production of this book:

The Hop Shop for the provision of dried flowers for the photographs. The shop is open every Saturday, and items are also available by mail order. The shop address is:

> The Hop Shop
> Castle Farm
> Shoreham
> Sevenoaks
> Kent
> TN14 7UB
> Telephone (09592) 3219

Joanna Sheen Ltd for the loan of the pot pourri, baskets, terracotta pots and other flower arranging items. The shop address is:

> Joanna Sheen Ltd
> 7 Lucius Street
> Torquay
> South Devon
> TQ2 5UW
> Telephone (0803) 201311

Suttons Seeds for kind permission to reproduce transparencies used in the A–Z section.

Mr and Mrs Gary Long for the use of their fireplace.